D0052651

WHO
MOVED MY
PULPIT?

Other Books by Thom S. Rainer

I Will
Autopsy of a Deceased Church
I Am a Church Member
The Millennials (coauthor)
Transformational Church (coauthor)
Simple Life (coauthor)
Essential Church (coauthor)
Vibrant Church (coauthor)
Raising Dad (coauthor)
Simple Church (coauthor)
The Unexpected Journey
The Unchurched Next Door
Surprising Insights from the Unchurched
Eating the Elephant (updated edition) (coauthor)
High Expectations
The Every Church Guide to Growth (coauthor)
The Bridger Generation
Effective Evangelistic Churches
The Church Growth Encyclopedia (coauthor)
Experiencing Personal Revival (coauthor)
Giant Awakenings
Biblical Standards for Evangelists (coauthor)
Eating the Elephant
The Book of Church Growth
Evangelism in the Twenty-First Century (editor)

WHO MOVED MY PULPIT?

LEADING CHANGE IN THE CHURCH

THOM S. RAINER

PUBLISHING GROUP

NASHVILLE, TENNESSEE

978-1-4336-4387-3

Published by B&H Publishing Group
Nashville, Tennessee

Dewey Decimal Classification: 254.5
Subject Heading: CHURCH ADMINISTRATION \ CHURCH
GROWTH \ CHURCH MEMBERSHIP

1 2 3 4 5 6 7 8 • 21 20 19 18 17 16

To
Team Rainer:

Amy Jordan
Jonathan Howe
Amy Thompson

Incredible Coworkers. Great Friends.

———

And always to

Nellie Jo

My Wife

Grateful to God for four decades of love and marriage.

CONTENTS

ACKNOWLEDGMENTS

One of the greatest desires of my life and ministry is to help church leaders move their churches to greater health.

But if most of our churches don't change, they will not be healthy. Many of them will die.

I am a blessed man to be able to hear about the state of our churches every day. I am grateful beyond words for the millions of men and women who join me and inform me at the ThomRainer.com blog, at our podcast, Rainer on Leadership, and at our mentoring ministries at ChurchAnswers.com. I hear from you every day. You are an incredible gift to me and to the body of Christ.

Thank you again to "Team Rainer" for all you do to make my world of ministry and my life a joy. You three—Amy Jordan, Jonathan ("The Voice") Howe, and Amy Thompson—are among the best and most joyous workers I know. I think you will understand how much I mean these words when you read the dedication page.

Ten years ago when I arrived at LifeWay, our book publishing arm, B&H Publishing, was struggling. Now it is the premier Christian book publisher. So many have contributed their leadership to this turnaround: Brad Waggoner; Selma Wilson; Eric Geiger; Cossy Pachares; and Jennifer Lyell. Jennifer is not only the leader of B&H trade books; she graciously agreed to be my editor as well.

I love and adore my family. I could not do anything of worth without them. I certainly couldn't write books. If my calculator is working, there are eighteen in my family at present count. There is my wife, Nellie Jo. There are my three sons and their wives: Sam and Erin; Art and Sarah; and Jess and Rachel. Seven years ago, I whined because I had no grandchildren. Today I have ten: Maggie, Bren, Joel, Nathaniel, Joshua, Canon, Will, Harper, and Collins. Number ten is due close to the release date of this book, so I don't know his or her name or gender yet.

You who read my blogs and books and listen to my podcasts are an incredible blessing. I don't deserve you, but I am thankful to God for you. I wrote my first book in 1989. This book is number twenty-six. I am so humbled because some of you have been with me on this journey from the onset.

You have likely heard me describe the state of churches in North America. Nearly nine out of ten are either declining, or they are growing more slowly than the communities in which they are located. In simple terms, 90 percent of our churches are losing ground in their respective communities.

Change is absolutely necessary in our churches. Major change is needed in most of them. But change is very difficult in most churches. Church members have become complacent and comfortable. Many church members have become highly change resistant.

The gospel is at stake. Eternal lives are at stake.

I pray this book on leading change in your church will be a catalyst to make a difference. I pray you and many leaders will read and study it together. And I pray you will be courageous to lead change no matter what the cost.

Welcome to the world of where pulpits get moved!

AN E-MAIL OF DESPERATION

Through social media, blog comments, e-mail, and other means, I receive several hundred requests for advice and counsel every month. I am humbled so many people would ask me for my counsel. But I am frustrated that I can't get to all of them.

But it was something about this e-mail that caught my attention. Indeed, there was something about this e-mail that prompted me to write this book.

Subject: A Plea for Help

Dr. Rainer—

I am a pastor and I'm about to give up. I have incredible seminary training where I learned about theology, the Bible, Greek, Hebrew, etc. But I know zero about dealing with conflict or leading the church to make some changes. Every time I try something, I get hit hard by critics and bullies.

My wife wants me to quit. She feels the pressure too. Some of the critics go after her, but most of her pain comes from watching me get hurt. She has cried herself to sleep too many nights. When we got married, she didn't know I would be a pastor one day. I didn't either. I'm not so sure I should be now.

I'm not sure how to ask for your help. I have too many questions. About all of my practical ministry training has come from the school of hard knocks and your blog and podcasts.

I guess what I need most is an A to Z plan on leading change in my church. Okay, I know that's asking too much. But maybe you could write your next book on this topic. I know many of us in ministry would benefit from it greatly. And I know I could share it with my elders so they would know what we are trying to do.

Yeah, this is a pretty bold request, but please prayerfully consider it. I'm not sure how long it takes you to write a book and get it on the shelves, but I know I don't have much time left. It looks like I could be facing three possibilities in the next couple of years. The likely change is we will continue to decline to the point the church can't afford to pay me a salary. Another possibility is I will get fired. Right now I have more supporters than adversaries, but I don't know how long it will last. The most likely option is I will just give up.

I am tired. My wife is tired. I never thought church leadership would be like this.

Please, please consider helping us church leaders understand how we can lead a church to change when we have so many obstacles.

Please help me. I think you can help a lot of us. Please help us before it's too late for many of us.

Thank you.

This book is for that pastor. This book is for all pastors seeking to lead their churches to change. This book is for church staff and lay leaders who want to make a positive contribution toward leading change in the church.

Now let's dive into the book and to that fateful Sunday when a pastor cried out:

"Who moved my pulpit?!"

CHAPTER 1

WHEN THE PULPIT GETS MOVED

Derek is the kind of guy you like to be around. He has a contagious laugh. He has a personality that draws people to him. And he is a pretty good leader.

He is also the pastor of Redeemer Church, a congregation of about 250 in the Midwest. Derek had been a pastor for twenty-three years, so he was no novice in leading churches. He had been at Redeemer Church for eight of those years, and he was respected and well liked by almost everyone in the congregation.

Derek understood the issue of change in established churches. As a leader, he was both methodical and incremental in his style. His approach to church leadership contributed significantly to his longer tenure in the church and in ministry in general. He did not fear conflict, but he felt too many church leaders create unnecessary conflict.

As pastor, Derek noticed a changed in his own ministry. His sermons were becoming more conversational in their approach and tone. He had not made that move as any grand strategic plan, but it was certainly a noticeable change from his style several years ago.

Derek surmised that the increased number of Millennials in the church had influenced his approach to preaching. These young adults included professionals in a growing technology company in the community, and others of them were coming from a nearby university.

It was obvious the Millennials preferred the conversational style of preaching. The most positive feedback to his sermons came when he shifted to the more informal approach. He was therefore certain his change in preaching style was a direct result of the increasing number of young adults in the church.

The pastor had also noticed the older congregants embracing his changing preaching style. He knew they were okay because his changes were incremental. He would preach a conversational message on one Sunday, and then go six weeks with his more formal and traditional approach. He slowly added the informal approach with greater frequency until the congregation became accustomed to it and comfortable with it.

Life and ministry were good for Derek. He could see staying at Redeemer Church for the rest of his ministry. He was so thankful that he had the total and unequivocal support of the church members.

At least he thought he did.

The Shocking Conflict

Derek had become increasingly uncomfortable with the pulpit he had used for all eight years at Redeemer Church. It had served him well when he was preaching more formally from a manuscript. But now he liked to get closer to the congregants. He saw the pulpit as a massive wooden barrier. It did not complement his newer preaching style. The pulpit, in his mind, cried out "traditional" and "formal" and "barrier."

He made a decision. The pulpit had to go.

On Friday of the next week, Derek asked the two custodians to move the massive old pulpit out. He replaced it with a new style of pulpit, a small lectern that was barely noticeable. *Now,* he thought, *the pulpit will complement my preaching style.*

In hindsight, the pastor now realizes he should have expected the explosion. And he admits he entered the worship service that Sunday with a bit of naiveté. He should have noticed the tension among some in the room. He should have seen the quiet conversations taking place before and after the services.

"I was both blind and blindsided," Derek confessed. "I did not notice the rumblings and the murmurings that Sunday morning. I guess I had become overconfident in my leadership style."

It began that Sunday afternoon.

First, there were a series of e-mails. All of them were negative, though the tone varied in intensity. One member of five years kindly suggested, "You should have given us a bit of forewarning." On the other extreme, a seventy-something member went right at the pastor: "What you have done is heretical! You ought to be ashamed of yourself. I think we need to call a vote of confidence about you."

The rest of the e-mail was another eight hundred words, but you get the point.

It was bad. Real bad.

Derek lost count of the e-mails, the meetings, and the phone calls that week. There was not a supportive voice among them. He stopped looking at Facebook after he saw several posts blasting him.

The pastor knew he had messed up. "I violated my own leadership principles," he said. "I have always led change incrementally in the established churches I served. I have tried not to surprise people. And I tried to get as much buy-in as possible." He paused for a moment. "I guess I had a period of temporary insanity," he concluded, but only partially in jest.

Derek knew what had to be done. It was too late, he surmised, to move the old pulpit back. The damage was done, and he really wanted to accentuate his more informal style. He determined he would offer the congregation a formal apology the next Sunday.

The pastor entered the worship center the following Sunday with some trepidation. He was not surprised to notice the huddled conversations. He was not surprised to feel the tension in the room. And he was not surprised to see many eyes glancing at the pulpit.

But he was *really* surprised at what he saw when he looked to the spot where the pulpit stood.

When he followed those glances toward the podium, Derek gave forth an audible gasp. Much to his surprise, he saw the reason for the murmurings this Sunday.

The old pulpit was back.

Many members contend that the following response really happened. In fact, they say it was so loud the entire congregation paused in quiet shock. Everyone said they heard it. In fact, some of the members said the pastor's question sounded more like a wail of agony.

"Who moved my pulpit?!"

The Aftermath

When I spoke with Derek about this incident, he was in his ninth year at Redeemer Church. He had survived the crisis, but barely.

"What is really disheartening," the pastor told me, "is that we've probably lost two years of effective momentum and ministry. We have been so inwardly focused dealing with this issue."

The pastor is still processing the issues. "On the one hand," he said, "I really can't believe the members were so preoccupied with something like a pulpit. I don't think they would have been as upset if I had preached heresy in my sermon. It just makes no sense."

We asked Derek what he did immediately after the old pulpit returned. His response was quiet but honest: "I sulked and pouted." We could tell there was still pain and regrets though two years had passed. "I thought I had earned a right to do something as small as moving a pulpit," he lamented. Derek took a deep breath and continued, "It wasn't as small as I thought it was."

First Failure: Not Praying

Derek was more than willing to conduct a diagnosis on this crisis. The pastor was an ongoing learner. Now that Redeemer Church had begun to regain momentum, he was glad to assess what went wrong.

"I can tell you easily what my first mess-up was," he began. "Every other time I have led change in this church, I have initiated it with prayer." We asked him to elaborate. "In all the other changes," he told us, "I spent about two weeks praying about it before I even mentioned it to someone else. This time I acted without prayer."

Derek was not done explaining. "I then asked a few of the true prayer warriors in the church to put it to prayer," he continued. "There are about eight of these men and women who have a heart and passion for intercessory prayer. I skipped over them this time."

He paused. It was as if Derek caught the severity of the mistake he had made. "I began in my own power," he said nearly in a whisper. "I had become so confident and cocky about my own leadership, I guess I thought I didn't need God this time."

"That's insane," the pastor said. "That's absolutely insane."

Second Failure: Not Assessing Unintended Consequences

Derek admitted he knew the old pulpit was an emotional issue for many church members. "What I can't believe," he said, "is that I never asked myself how people would respond to this change. I should have known better."

One of the principles of leadership in any organization, particularly a local church, is *the law of unintended consequences*. It points out that *any significant change in an organization will have reactions that extend well beyond the change itself.*

The pastor had failed to consider the consequences of moving the pulpit. Even though he knew there were deep and long-standing emotional ties to the pulpit, he did not consider how the reactions might impact the church. Derek thought he could win the day with the power of his personality.

Third Failure: Not Communicating

A pastor once asked me how much he should communicate an important issue in the church. My response was "a lot more than you're communicating now." To be clear, I did not know how much he was actually communicating to the congregation. I simply know that if something is important to the church, it really cannot be over-communicated.

Derek never communicated about this issue to the church. He never explained his rationale. He did not share with the people about his evolving preaching style.

He just did it.

And he paid a great price.

Fourth Failure: Not Dealing with People Issues

"If I had to assess my biggest blunder," Derek shared, "it would be my failure to deal with people issues. I messed up on the front end, in the middle, and in the aftermath."

Though I thought I knew where he was headed with this discussion, I asked him to elaborate.

"I did not get buy-in on the front end," he responded. "I know who our key influencers are in the church. I just bulldozed ahead." Derek then told me where he fell short further in the process.

"I had my opportunity when I walked in the worship center that morning," he began. "Because I was so focused on myself, I had that visceral reaction. I cried out, 'Who Moved My Pulpit?!' I should have taken time to admit my errors that morning, and to share with the congregation why I changed the pulpits."

I anticipated his conversation about the aftermath. He confirmed it. "Yep, I really blew it in the days and weeks that followed," he confessed. "I was getting beaten up on social media, by e-mail, in meetings, and by telephone. Man, church members can really be mean. But instead of leading, I went into emotional retreat."

That brings us to the fifth failure Derek acknowledged.

Fifth Failure: Not Modeling Positive Leadership

"I was ready to leave the church," he told me emphatically. "Make no mistake about it. I wanted out!"

Well, my conversation with Derek was two years after the incident. He obviously did not leave. I was curious to know more.

"My attitude stunk for about three months," he admitted. "I wanted out, and I was mad at my church. I went into a mode of pouting and withdrawal.

"Toward the end of that third month," he said, "I was reading Nehemiah in my quiet time. I became aware, painfully aware, how much opposition, threats, and problems he had. But he was a positive model of leadership. He provided the role model the Jews needed to build the wall around Jerusalem.

"It hit me like a sack of bricks in the head," he said metaphorically. "Church members were looking to me and my example. I had to change first. I had to get my head screwed on straight. I had to have the right attitude. Healthy change had to start with me."

Leading Change in the Church

We will hear from Derek again later. He made big mistakes. He admitted his poor leadership cost the church two years of momentum.

But there's another side to this story. It's the story of church members who are so focused on "my needs" and "my desires" that they resist change at every turn.

To that perspective we now turn.

Diagnostic and Study Questions

1. Why can something seemingly as minor as changing pulpits create conflict in the church?

2. Read Nehemiah 1:4–11. What does Nehemiah's prayer tell us about the relationship between prayer and change?

3. Pastors and other church leaders tell us that church members are more critical than ever today. What has changed in the last twenty years to bring on this negative reality?

4. What can we learn from Philippians 2:1–11 about the right attitudes for church leaders and church members?

CHAPTER 2

FIVE KINDS OF UNMOVABLE CHURCH MEMBERS

There is a reason Pastor Derek became frustrated.

Sure, he readily admits he made some mistakes. Indeed, he wishes he had a do-over for the pulpit incident. He knows he will be remembered for the exclamatory shout: "Who moved my pulpit?!"

But it's not all Derek's fault. After all, it was just a pulpit. It was not some heretical teaching. It really was just a pulpit.

Pastors and other church leaders make mistakes. Church members often exacerbate them.

So let's look at these unmovable church members. There are many different kinds of stubborn members, but most of them fall into these five categories.

The Deniers

I was helping my son, Sam, on a consultation in a mid-western state. My primary job was to interview longer-term members. The evidence of decline was clear and disturbing. Worship attendance was down from 350 to 180 in five years. The church was marching down a death spiral.

One of my interviewees was a lady in her seventies. She had been at the church for nearly half a century. I asked her what she thought was behind the church's decline. Even after three decades of church consulting, I was surprised by her response: "Our church is not declining."

I showed her the attendance graph. She denied its accuracy. I asked her if she noticed more open seats in the worship center. She did not. I inquired if she knew anyone who had left the church. She could not recall.

I gave up.

Denial. Total and complete denial.

The denier is one of the most difficult to lead in change because he or she does not think anything needs changing. The church is just fine the way it is, and there is no motivation to do things differently.

Denial is the fastest path to death.

The Entitled

The entitled church member treats the church more like a country club than a church. They view their financial offerings as dues to get perks and privileges. They make pastors and other church leaders cringe when they say, "You do know we pay your salary."

The entitled church member is the antithesis of the biblical church member described in 1 Corinthians 12. The apostle Paul describes that type of church member as giving, functioning, and sacrificing. He or she is a member of the body of Christ for the greater good of the church. Others come first.

An entitled church member expects *his* worship style. She expects *her* color of the rooms and temperature in the worship center. They expect *their* pastor to jump when they call. After all, they think, it's *our* church. We should be able to get what *we* want.

The entitled church member resists change constantly. These church members do not want anything that upsets their way of doing church to be introduced to the congregation. Church is about their perks, their desires, and their comfort.

Biblical church members will gladly accept change to reach people with the gospel, and to bring glory to God. Entitled church members are in churches to get their needs met. Change is thus difficult and sometimes futile.

The Blamers

Blamers would rather blame than be obedient: "It's the pastor's fault. If our pastor would be a better leader, our church would be so much better."

It's the fault of culture: "Our society is so messed up. We can't expect to really do anything well when the world is against us. Even our own community does not like us. It's an uphill battle."

It's the fault of the new churches in town: "I don't understand why these new churches keep starting in this community. We already have a church almost on every block. If they would stay out of this town, we could all grow. But they are taking the new people and some of the members of churches already here. Something should be done about those new churches."

It's the fault of other church members: "That was a great sermon today, pastor. I hope some of the people in the church who need to hear got the message. We've got too many people who just aren't pulling their weight in this church."

The blamers resist change because they do not need to change, at least from their perspective. The problems all reside with other people and other situations. They don't see anything wrong with themselves.

Blamers will blame. Blamers do not want to change.

The Critics

The critics are like the blamers because they also believe the problems in the church are someone else's fault. But the critics are even worse, because they drain pastors and other church leaders of their energies.

Sometimes critics are direct. They will tell you directly about their feelings. They will tell you face-to-face or in the form of some written communication.

Other critics are more cowardly. They go to Facebook or some other social media to air their grievances. They not only spread their venom, they draw others into it as well. I know of too many pastors who ultimately left their churches because they were castigated so severely on social media.

Perhaps the worst of the critics are the "PAST" critics. PAST is an acronym for "People are saying that . . ." It is the worst form of criticism because the critics will not own up to the criticism. These critics are cowards who try to assign blame to some anonymous person or persons for the problems they articulate. Of course, almost all of the time, the "people who are saying that . . ." are the ones who voice the issue at the onset. There are no other "people."

This type of critic combines negativity with deception to get his or her point across.

They are among the first who will voice a complaint when change is initiated. They are difficult, devious, and deceptive change resisters.

The Confused

The confused are often well-intending church members. They really do view some things as more important than they were intended. The outcry by church members over the new pulpit is a classic example of the confused who resist change. They see the pulpit as something sacred in itself. To change the pulpit is therefore a sacred violation.

Sometimes the confused includes those who want to hang on to some tradition for their own sense of security and comfort. They may sincerely believe the tradition to be vitally important. They don't see that there is no intrinsic or doctrinal value in these items. I have worked with a number of churches that have a group of these change resisters regarding the order of service. If the offertory is moved in the order of worship, someone may feel like heresy is in the midst.

In simple terms, the confused give highest priorities to those things that are not high priority. Belief in the bodily resurrection is a tenet that cannot be compromised. Skipping the doxology one week will not result in immediate damnation.

The confused must shed their confusion to be receptive to change. It's not always an easy task.

Meet the World of God's Possibilities

The first part of this chapter may discourage you. It may frighten you. It may even dissuade you from leading forward.

But there is hope, God's hope.

I know there is a hope because I've seen so-called hopeless cases become incredible breakout stories. I know there is hope because I've seen churches in rural areas with negative population growth become dynamic forces for God's work in their communities.

I know the story of an established church in Maryland that had more sacred cows than any church I can recall. Attendance was not on a free fall; it was worse. The decline was gradual. In fact it was so gradual that the members did not see it.

Think about a church declining from four hundred in worship attendance to three hundred in ten years. Attendance was thus declining by only ten people a year. That's less than a one-person decline every month. It's virtually invisible to those who are present on a regular basis. But it's a 25 percent decline in a decade.

The established church in Maryland experienced that same gradual erosion. The membership included large numbers of the deniers, the entitled, and the critics. Pastors had come and gone quickly over the past twenty years; most of them were in a hurry to leave. The church went through three pastors in seven years, including the interim periods.

Word spread that this church was a "preacher-eater." Any sane leader would not ever consider going to the church. It could destroy your ministry and hurt your family.

But Marcus did accept the call to the church. He has now been there five years. It has not been easy. He had his moments where he questioned his own sanity. The deniers were the first to discourage him. The entitled and the critics quickly followed.

The story at this point is good. Very good.

Attendance is on a rebound for the first time in more than a decade. New discipleship and evangelistic ministries are beginning to make a difference. The reputation of the church in the community is now positive.

For sure, there are the naysayers: the deniers; the entitled; and the critics in particular. But their voices aren't nearly as dominant now as those who are excited about the direction of the church. No, things aren't perfect. But they are so much better.

A Roadmap for Leading Change

When you begin to analyze how Marcus led the church, eight clear patterns begin to emerge. In many ways, these patterns become a roadmap for leading change. No, it is not a "plug-and-play" program. No, it is not a quick-fix solution. But it is a biblically sound and commonsensical approach to leading change. And it is something that has obviously been used successfully in many churches.

I am incredibly excited to share this information with you who are leaders in your church. And though I expect pastors and other church staff leaders to be the primary readers of this book, I hope there is a good representation of lay leaders as well. I want all of you to see these possibilities of change in your church. I pray all of you will see the possibilities of breakout ministry and growth in your congregations.

The roadmap has eight stages. Though they are not perfectly sequential, there is a sense of orderliness to this process. It's often difficult to proceed to the next stage until the previous stages have been processed.

Here is a simple overview of the eight-stage roadmap for leading change in your church:

Stop and Pray

The crucial foundational issue often
neglected in leading change

Confront and Communicate a Sense of Urgency

Facing and sharing the bru-
tal facts with the congregation

Build an Eager Coalition

Most churches have at least a few members ready to move forward.

Become a Voice and Vision of Hope

Members look to leaders for hope and possibilities

Deal with People Issues

The courage to handle people blockage, both staff and church members

Move from an Inward Focus to an Outward Focus

Steadily moving the church beyond mostly focusing on herself

Pick Low-Hanging Fruit

Clear victories are necessary to sustain positive momentum.

Implement and Consolidate Change
Gospel urgency never ends.
Complacency is always a danger.

The Time Is Now

The bad news is clear. Nine out of ten churches in North America are losing ground in the communities in which they are located. They are declining or growing more slowly than their respective communities.

The good news is clear as well. More churches are indeed breaking out. More churches are indeed revitalizing. What seemed to be an impossible situation in many congregations is now a showcase for God's possibilities.

The New Testament is an action story. It is the story of the gospel moving forward. It is the story of moving obstacles as the gospel moves forward.

Too many congregations today are stuck; they are not moving forward. The Great Commission of Matthew 28:18–20 is about moving forward. At its essence, the Great Commission is about going. Such going requires forward movement, and it requires removing the obstacles that will hinder the progress.

You are about to enter the world of God's possibilities. This book is not about an expert sharing his opinion. This book rather is a collection of stories of how God has used leaders to move toward change and progress. It is the story of the work of God in God's churches.

My assignment is simple. I am the observer of these real examples who then shares the essence of what transpired. I am particularly focused on sharing transferable truths so you can lead your church to change.

The time is now.

The time is now for obedience to the Great Commission.

The time is now for leading unhealthy churches to health.

The time is now for you.

We begin the process in the next chapter with the non-negotiable foundation of prayer.

Diagnostic and Study Questions

1. Give a possible example of how each type of unmovable church member could hinder growth and health in your church: the denier; the entitled; the blamers; the critics; and the confused.

2. Using 1 Corinthians 12 as the model, compare and contrast a functioning church member to an entitled church member.

3. Review the eight stages of the roadmap for change. Where do you think most churches have the greatest challenges?

4. Why is it crucial to include verse 18 in the Great Commission passage of Matthew 28:18–20?

CHAPTER 3

STOP . . . AND PRAY

I know what you are doing here.

Okay. I'm not omniscient.

I think I know why you are here.

You are in a church, a church you would like to see change. You know that some level of change is needed because you should be reaching more people with the gospel. You want the church to have a greater impact on your community. You would rejoice if most of the church members acted like true disciples of Christ.

You are here because you either want to lead change or be a part of leading change.

But there is something about people like you and me. We want to see tangible results right away. We want to be as active as possible. Leading change for us means moving forward.

That might be the biggest mistake you could make.

Before leading change, it is time to stop. It is time to stop and pray.

Back to the Past Before Moving to the Future

I bet you love the book of Nehemiah. It's an action-oriented book of the Bible. It's about getting the job done. It's about a fast pace of work. It's about fast-forward leadership.

You remember the story, don't you? Nehemiah hears that the wall of Jerusalem is broken into bits and pieces. He hears that the solid wooden gates have been burned to ashes. Nehemiah is devastated to hear these heartbreaking stories of his homeland.

You remember what he does, don't you? He gets permission from King Artaxerxes to go back to Jerusalem, and he immediately starts leading a coalition to build the wall. That's the story, right?

Wrong.

We who are action-oriented and ready to see change sooner than later often overlook or forget Nehemiah's first step. It's right there in Nehemiah 1:4: "When I heard these words, I sat down and wept. I mourned for a number of days, fasting and praying before the God of heaven."

Did you get that?

Nehemiah fasted and prayed *for a number of days* before taking steps to lead change. He knew he could not lead this effort without the wisdom, strength, and courage of God.

Nehemiah prayed. He had to do so. So do you.

You and God

Perhaps your church has been struggling. Maybe you know change needs to take place, but you are not entirely certain what the nature of the change needs to be.

You need to pray for God's wisdom.

You are facing the likelihood of critics and naysayers. You have felt the barbs of their words before. They have caused you to retreat. You can't retreat this time.

You need to pray for God's courage.

Leading change in the church is impossible in your own power. It can be both redundant and exhausting. There will be days where you will wonder if it's worth it. You will be worn out.

You need to pray for God's strength.

You might have a special place you can go to be alone with God for a few days. You may not have the opportunity to leave and go somewhere, but you know where you can go for an hour or so a day to pray about you, your church, and the need for change.

More than twenty years ago, before multisite churches were cool, I tried to lead my church to become multisite. The logic was simple, I thought. We were landlocked. There was no availability of contiguous land. Why not start a second site a few miles away in a fast-growing area?

Seemingly out of the blue, I received a call from a Methodist pastor. His church, just a few miles south of us, was growing rapidly. They were moving to a new location, but they needed a buyer for their property. They would take an under market offer if they could get a church in that site.

It gets better. The facilities were outstanding, only seven years old. It was as if the site was ready and waiting for us.

I took a few key leaders to the site. I shared with them my enthusiasm. We could afford the purchase price. It was just so obvious.

The next week I went to a leadership meeting. I expected to be greeted with words of affirmation and excitement. I expected them to be on board fully to move forward to propose the idea to the entire congregation. Instead I heard these words.

"We've never seen a model like this. How do we know if we are doing it right?"

"There are no examples of multisite churches in the Bible. We could be committing heresy."

"We need to use this money for things at this church. The people here have needs too."

Sigh. You get the picture.

I guess my despondency was noticeable the next day. Frances noticed. You need to understand Frances Mason. She was an incredible woman of prayer. When she died a few years ago, I felt like I lost one of my best friends.

Of course, Frances did not hesitate to ask me what my problem was. She was bold in prayer and bold in person. I explained to her the sequence of events related to the failed effort of the new site. She showed no pity. Instead, she simply said, "I suppose you haven't talked to God about it."

I swallowed hard. I didn't have to give Frances a verbal answer. She knew.

Leading effective change in your church without prayer will not work. And it's not very smart either.

You and God and Someone Else

Because of my failed leadership, we did not get the facilities owned by the Methodist church. It sold quickly to another congregation.

But I still had to deal with our shortage of space. I still had to lead change, but now I wasn't sure what the change would be.

This time, however, I learned my lesson. I enlisted Frances to join me in prayer. She asked a few others to join her to pray about this matter.

We would soon get our answer. Our church was able to find several adjoining storefronts in a retail center. Within a few months we had our second site, and several people started joining us there.

I am sure I did plenty of things wrong in this change leadership process. I simply did not have a model to follow. But the greatest blunder I made was beginning in my own power. I was stupid enough to believe I could lead in my own strength.

Over the course of three decades of working with church leaders, I know there is a strong desire to press forward. Depending on the definition, as many as nine out of ten churches need some serious changes. Leaders naturally have a growing impatience to see progress. There is a tendency among many of us to move forward without prayer.

Hear me clearly. I have never seen successful and sustaining change take place in a church without prayer. Never. Not once.

You are likely a leader in your church. A pastor. A church staff person. An elder, deacon, or other lay leader.

You desire to be an effective leader for change in your congregation. *Please* note these words once more: I have never seen successful and sustaining change take place in a church without prayer.

Never.

It is incumbent upon you to put the matter to prayer for a period of time. It is incumbent upon you to ask others to join you in a season of prayer for the change initiative.

Nehemiah began with prayer.

So should you.

Pray for Wisdom

Change means you are leading the congregation to a preferred future. Pause for a moment and see if you agree with the preceding statement. Assuming you do, there is a word in the sentence that needs a bit of discussion: *future*.

Obviously, leading change in the church means something will look differently in the future. This creates one big challenge. We can't see the future. Sure we can anticipate the future. Perhaps we can be pretty accurate about the near-term future.

But we really don't know the future.

That is why change leaders pray for wisdom. You are praying to the One who knows all eternity. He certainly knows our temporal future.

Have you been through a major change initiative, only to be surprised by how many times you were surprised? It never works out just like we anticipated. There is a good explanation for that reality.

We really don't know the future.

Praying for wisdom means you are asking God to lead you through this unknown future. You are admitting you do not and will not have all the answers. He does.

How do we know God will give us this wisdom? We know because he promises he will if we ask. Look at this incredible promise from James 1:5: "If any of you lacks wisdom, he should ask God, who gives to all generously and without criticizing, and it will be given to him."

We ask God for wisdom. He gives it to us. It is really that basic.

Prayer for Courage

Some time ago, I did a survey to find out what type of petty arguments church leaders had experienced. The responses were quite revealing, definitely discouraging, but a bit humorous. Here are fifteen of my "favorites":

1. Argument over the appropriate length of the worship pastor's beard.
2. Fight over whether or not to build a children's playground or to use the land for a cemetery.
3. A deacon accusing another deacon of sending an anonymous letter, and deciding to settle the matter in the parking lot.
4. A church dispute of whether or not to install restroom stall dividers in the women's restroom.
5. A church argument and vote to decide if a clock in the worship center should be removed.

6. A forty-five-minute heated argument over the type of filing cabinet to purchase: black or brown; two, three, or four drawers.
7. A fight over which picture of Jesus to put in the foyer.
8. A petition to have all church staff clean-shaven.
9. A dispute over whether the worship leader should have his shoes on during the service.
10. A big church argument over the discovery that the church budget was off $0.10. Someone finally gave a dime to settle the issue.
11. A dispute in the church because the Lord's Supper had cranberry/grape juice instead of grape juice.
12. Business meeting arguments about whether the church should purchase a weed eater or not. It took two business meetings to resolve it.
13. Arguments over what type of green beans the church should serve.
14. Two different churches reported fights over the type of coffee they served. In one of the churches, they moved from Folgers to a stronger Starbucks brand. In the other church, they simply moved to a stronger blend. Members left the church in the latter example.
15. Major conflict when the youth borrowed a Crockpot that had not been used for years.

My point in listing these silly arguments is to remind church leaders that any kind of change can bring out the worst in some church members. Significant change can be really difficult.

You will be criticized if you lead change. It could really get tough at times.

You need courage to move forward.

You need to pray for courage.

Pray for Strength

Leading change in most churches is like eating an elephant: one bite at a time. The pace can be painfully slow. It is easy to grow weary in the process and of the process.

Have you heard of a leader who was "coasting"? It's not a very complimentary term. It means that the leader has really given up.

Coasting requires no effort.

Coasting avoids conflict.

Coasting is for leaders who have stopped leading.

But true change leaders expend a tremendous amount of effort. They face challenges and conflicts regularly. They have discouraging setbacks.

They can really grow tired.

That's why those leading change must pray for strength. Effective change leadership in the church will not take place in human power; it can only come from God.

Of course, God promises strength to those who ask. There are so many scriptural promises to that effect. This passage in Isaiah 40:29–31 is always a favorite: "He gives strength to the weary and strengthens the powerless. Youths may faint and grow weary, and young men stumble and fall, but those who trust in the LORD will renew their strength; they will soar on wings like eagles; they will run and not grow weary; they will walk and not faint."

You need to pray for strength.

Time to Lead Change

Prayer is not an option in leading change in the church; it is foundational.

You are not smart enough to lead change. You need to pray for wisdom.

You are not brave enough to lead change. You need to pray for courage.

You are not strong enough to lead change. You need to pray for strength.

Please pardon me for being redundant. But I will say it one more time. *I have never seen successful and sustaining change take place in a church without prayer.*

Now it is time to lead change in your church. A challenging task lies ahead. You must confront some not-so-pleasant facts.

You will be fine though. You are moving forward with God's wisdom, courage, and strength.

Diagnostic and Study Questions

1. Explain what Nehemiah asked of God in the first chapter of the book. How does that relate to change in the church?

2. Explain the promise of God for wisdom in James 1:5. What does it mean that God will "give to all without criticizing"?

3. Name some potential blockages to change in your church. Try to assess their root causes.

4. Why is it so important to pray for wisdom, courage, and strength in leading change in the church?

CHAPTER 4

CONFRONT AND COMMUNICATE A SENSE OF URGENCY

I love beaches.

I am particularly fond of beaches in Florida on the panhandle and in southwest Florida. There is just something about the sugar-white sand, the emerald water, the bright sun, and the blue sky.

I simply love the beaches.

It had been many years since I had visited one particular beach. In fact the gap in time had been from my pre-teen years to my early thirties. But I wanted to go back. I wanted to see the beach of my childhood. So Nellie Jo and I made the journey.

Let me take a brief moment to describe the beach of my childhood. It was huge. I confirmed with others that its vastness was not just the perspective of a child. It really was big. I guess I remember the big sand dunes the most. They were massive mountains of white sand with light vegetation.

They were absolutely beautiful. I couldn't wait to return.

So, twenty years later, I arrived at the beach with anticipation and excitement. But what I saw was like a kick in the gut.

The sand dunes were gone, completely gone. The beach was half its size of twenty years earlier. Even the sun seemed less bright since it did not have as much white sand to reflect.

I was totally bummed.

As I was walking on the beach, I saw a man come out of one of the older homes. I asked him if he had been a resident for a while. He smiled and responded, "Thirty-four years." I then asked him the obvious question: What happened to the beach?

His response was shocking: "What do you mean? It's pretty much the same as it has always been."

I would later learn that overdevelopment and beach erosion had taken its toll on the beach. But to those who see the beach every day, the change had been incremental. They didn't see the "before and after" of two decades like I did.

They really didn't see reality.

So it is in many churches. The members don't see the need to make changes because they don't see reality. They don't see the decline. They don't see the worn facilities. They don't notice that the church is not reaching unbelievers as it once did.

And, because they don't see the decline and deterioration, they see no need to change. Such is one of the main reasons leaders have difficulty leading churches to change. Why should we change if there is really no need for change?

Your role as a change leader has three major components. First, you have to lead the congregation to face reality. Then you have to communicate that reality and the steps needed to move forward again and again. Finally, you must communicate with a sense of urgency. Where do you begin? Here are some simple steps to take.

Face the Numbers

Some church leaders and members have grown weary of numbers and church statistics. They feel like numbers have taken on too much importance, that they have become ends in themselves.

I get that.

But don't throw the metaphorical baby out with the bath water. Numbers can be helpful for accountability and for facing reality. If your church has declined in worship attendance from 300 to 175 in ten years, something is going wrong. If your church used to reach thirty people a year with the gospel, but no one has been reached in three years, something is wrong.

Numbers are not the goal, but they can point our churches to reality. They can engender accountability. They can be helpful.

Does your church keep records? Does it have the past ten years of data? Can you get the following information?

- Average worship attendance the past ten years.
- Number of conversions for each of the past ten years.
- Average attendance in your groups or Sunday school each year for the past ten years.

That's it. While it may help to have a few more statistical categories, these three will tell a major story. And if you have just average worship attendance, you still can find some enlightening trends.

Get Outside Eyes for Your Facilities

Find someone who has never been to your church. That's usually a pretty easy task. Ask them to assess all of the church's facilities, from the signage to the parking lot to the exterior to the interior. Ask them to take copious notes. Perhaps you can even pay them a small stipend for the effort.

Actually, let me make it easier on you. Go to ThomRainer. com and get the free facility audit. Have the guest complete it. Make certain you ask them to be perfectly transparent and truthful, even if the process is a bit painful.

After they have looked over all of your facilities and grounds, take the information and assess it yourself. Perhaps you bring in a few key leaders. It's time to face the reality of what guests see when they come to your church.

I can anticipate the objections. Why should I do that? In the scope of eternity, what's the big deal about a church's facilities? After all, some churches around the world are just huts or mud buildings. Some churches have no facilities.

Imagine for a moment, however, that a young couple visits your church. They are not Christians, but they have a newborn baby, and they are beginning to ask questions about the Christian faith. They show up at your church. What do they see?

If they see an unkempt and rundown facility, they may have second thoughts about leaving their young child in the church nursery. They may wonder why a group of Christians have such a careless attitude.

They decide not to return.

Indeed, they decide that your church is representative of all churches, so they go nowhere. They don't hear the gospel. They don't connect with other believers.

They just leave.

Is that important to you?

Get Outside Eyes for Your Worship Services

The same rationale applies to worship services. You want guests to have a positive experience. You want them to return. You desire for them to hear the gospel and to connect with believers.

Ask an outsider, someone who has never been to your church, to attend a worship service. Ask them to observe and take notes if possible. Ask them to be honest and blunt. You want to learn. You want to improve.

Let me give you a good example. It's a true story. A first-time guest came to the church at the request of the pastor. She was to observe carefully, then write a brief report.

There was one comment that had no explanation: "I knew twenty minutes into the service, I would not want to return." The pastor called her and asked her to elaborate.

"It happened during the stand and greet time," she began. "I'm an introvert, so I don't usually like being asked to greet people I don't know. But I went along with it; I had an assignment to do, and I wanted to make the best of it."

The pastor waited as she paused, and then continued: "Even though I'm an introvert, I made a point of seeking people out. I looked folks straight in the eye," she said. "And you know what happened?" she asked rhetorically. "No one greeted me. They avoided eye contact. They were greeting people they knew by first name."

She then spoke softly, "No one said a word to me. No one. I felt so out of place and alone. I would not come back."

Wow. "I would not come back."

I encourage church leaders to have a "secret guest" twice a year. Pay them a small stipend if necessary. Ask them to report back honestly and bluntly. It will help your church face reality. And it may lead your church to make changes.

Communicate the Reality with Urgency

It does absolutely no good for only a few people to know about the realities of the church. Your church members need to know. Your church members must know.

Take time to share the numbers. Tell the stories of those who have looked at the church's facilities. Share the experiences of the secret guest who came to the church. Share the information clearly and factually. Hold nothing back. Share the good and the bad.

Your church members may not receive bad news well, especially if they have been in denial. They may offer excuses for the challenges of the church. They may point to numerous ministries in the church as proof the church is moving forward. In other words, church members often view activities as evidence the church is making a difference.

But often in many of our churches, activities mean the church is just, well, busy.

Leading change in the church means you must communicate the reality of the true health of the church.

When 90 percent of American congregations are either declining or growing more slowly than their respective communities, we know our churches are losing ground. We know something is not right.

But it is not just a matter of communicating reality; it is communicating that reality with a sense of urgency.

Too many of our church members treat their congregation as a religious country club. They pay their dues and expect to be served. It is the "me-first" attitude that is endemic in the unhealthy churches in America.

We must communicate the urgency of the gospel. We must remind people again and again that John 14:6 is true, that Christ is the only way of salvation. We must tell the hopeless that they have hope in Christ. We are running out of time, and we can't do church business as usual.

It is time for our churches to wake up. It is time to lead change in our churches.

The Power of Repetition

As you lead change, you confront the realities of your church. You communicate those realities with the congregation. And you communicate them with a sense of urgency.

So what happens next?

You repeat the process again. And again. And again.

As a leader, you are constantly confronting realities, communicating realities, and communicating the urgency of the moment. You may tire of the redundancy. You may think it's time to be quiet for a season.

But it's not. You communicate. And then communicate. And then communicate again.

Change or Die

Several years ago, a physician gave a man in his late fifties a warning. The X-rays showed his lungs to be scarred from years of smoking. The doctor had seen such situations many times. Lung cancer or emphysema would follow. Either path would lead to death, often a cruel and painful death.

But the doctor offered the man hope. He did not have cancer at the moment. He did not have emphysema. The damage to his lungs, the physician explained, could be at least partly reversed if he just stopped smoking. If he did not, his life would likely be cut short.

The choice was simple: change or die.

To be certain, the change would be difficult. Anyone who has kicked the smoking habit will tell you that.

But the decision itself was basic: change or die.

The man chose to keep smoking. He made no attempt to kick his habit. And he died at the relatively young age of sixty-two.

I know this story well because that man was my dad. He did not live long enough to get to know his grandchildren. He had so much to offer, but he chose the path of not changing. And so he died.

In a similar story, a church in our area was in a state of rapid decline and I offered to help lead them toward greater health. But I told them that they could not reverse years of decline without significant changes. They were a totally inwardly focused congregation.

When I mentioned just a few of the needed changes, the members balked. They had never done it that way before. They decided they were okay just as they were.

They had a clear choice: change or die. They chose to die. Indeed in this case, death came quicker than anyone would have anticipated. The church ceased to exist in just a matter of months. Death came quickly.

It takes courage to be a change leader in the church. Opposition and resistance often come frequently and fiercely. But too much is at stake to do otherwise.

Confront the realities.

Communicate the realities.

And communicate with a sense of urgency.

The choice is simple: change or die.

Diagnostic and Study Questions

1. How would you describe the path of your church the past ten years? Is it one of health and urgency, or is it one of steady decline? How can you best answer these questions?

2. If you were a first-time guest at your church, what do you think your experience would be?

3. How does John 14:6 relate to communicating with a sense of urgency?

4. What are some ways realities can best be communicated in your church?

CHAPTER 5

BUILD AN EAGER COALITION

It was an incredibly inspirational church business meeting.

Yes, you read correctly. The business meeting was upbeat, festive, and joyous.

Most of you may be wondering if I was not in my right mind when I attended the meeting. After all, most church business meetings fit one of two descriptors: boring or divisive. It almost seems like an alternative reality to use words like upbeat, festive, and joyous to describe the usually dreary events, but the description is on target.

Let me back up a couple of years and take you to that business meeting. The church had a reputation of being vicious to pastors. The previous five pastors did not make it to their third year. The current pastor had just passed his second year, and people in the community were waiting for his exit to take place sooner than later.

That anticipation became even stronger when word got out of the changes that would be proposed in the business meeting. The entire worship center would be renovated. The organ would be donated to another church, the same organ that had been donated by the most prominent family in the church.

The pews were to be removed and replaced with chairs. By the way, each pew had a plaque on the end in honor or memory of a church member.

The carpet would be removed. The walls would be painted with a different color than the dead gray that is there now. The stage would be extended seven feet.

And here's the coup de grace. The pulpit would be replaced. The pulpit had been with the church since its founding over 110 years ago. It was the same massive pulpit that had been generously donated by a founding family whose descendants were still in the church. In fact, more than sixty church members were tied relationally to the family.

I anticipated the cry to be worse than, "Who moved my pulpit?!" I really expected someone to mention doing something over his or her dead body.

I walked into the packed worship center for the business meeting on a Sunday evening. I expected palpable tension. Instead the environment seemed to be one of excitement and anticipation. I expected frowns and huddled groups. Instead I saw smiles and open conversations.

The moderator approached the podium and called the meeting to order. Before I could blink he asked the pastor to present the exciting changes that would be recommended.

Before the meeting, I expected the pastor not to survive the evening. Instead he approached the podium with a round of thunderous applause.

Maybe I *was* in an alternative universe.

The pastor presented slides showing the future worship center. He spoke with warmth about how grateful he was for those who had guided him through this process. With each subsequent slide and comment, you could tell the excitement was building.

He did not hold anything back. The pastor spoke about all of the changes, including the pulpit. The sacred pulpit.

The pastor stopped. His presentation was over. The moderator asked for questions. There were four. That's right: only four questions. And none of the questions were antagonistic.

The question was called. The vote to move forward took place. It was unanimous. According to the historical lore of the church, there had never been a unanimous vote. Until now. Until all these sacred cows were sacrificed.

The entire business meeting took thirty-four minutes. The meeting concluded with twenty minutes of prayer and songs of praise.

It was unreal. Totally unreal.

I had to wait almost an hour. So many members wanted to talk to the pastor and pat his back. I waited patiently. He saw me headed toward him. I saw the weary smile on his face.

I didn't hesitate. "How did you do it?" I asked. "How did you get such massive change approved in less than an hour?"

Before he responded, I saw the weariness on his face. I saw something beyond what had just taken place.

"It didn't take less than an hour," he said softly. "I have been meeting with people for ten months. I have been in hundreds and hundreds of hours of meetings."

I simply shook his hand, and he left victoriously but tired, very tired.

He paid the price to get the change approved. He indeed built an eager coalition.

Lone Ranger Leaders Won't Get It Done

On the surface, leading major change alone is tempting. I've been there and done that. We think on the basis of our personalities, intellect, and leadership acumen we can do it alone.

We can't.

Yes, I know that some pastors move interminably slow when making decisions. They wait until they've spoken to everyone. They are hesitant to make the move. They fear the consequences. They try to avoid conflict, so they delay making decisions. For certain, that type of church leader is not ready to lead change.

So we often move to the other extreme. We don't bother getting buy-in. We fail to listen to others' ideas and opinions. We loathe if we have to change something because we heard a good suggestion.

So we go it alone.

Lone Ranger leaders only have only opinion: their own. And if they start having challenges and problems, they have no one to turn to because they have no one in their coalition for change. In the South, we often said "he got hung out to dry."

Perhaps there was a day when change was relatively slow enough that one person could be fairly effective in leading change. But as we experience technological, societal, cultural, and economic change faster than ever, the solo act just does not cut it.

Lone Ranger leaders are not good change leaders.

The Sinkhole Committee

Have you ever seen a sinkhole? They are caused by some form of collapse of the surface layer. I lived in Florida where sinkholes are common. Much of the land consists of carbonate rock that can dissolve over time. The sinkholes can swallow cars, people, and homes. If something goes into a sinkhole, you probably won't see it again.

I was serving as a pastor of a church where a small group of church members were persistent in pushing through some change that all of us on the church staff knew would be harmful to the church. The solution to our problem came from one of the oldest members in the church.

He didn't speak much, but when he did, people listened. He came into my study one weekday and said he wanted to talk to me about "the stupid idea that group has." I was immediately put at ease since he recognized the absurdity of the idea himself.

"Take my advice, pastor," he said. "Give it to the church council to handle. We've called them the sinkhole committee for years. Once they get ahold of an idea, they will discuss it forever, and you won't ever hear about it again."

My senior church member was right. I informed the small group I was turning their proposal over to the church council. They seemed pleased I was moving forward.

The church council deliberated on the idea for almost two years. One of the leaders of the group proposing the idea died. The idea died soon thereafter as well. It was indeed a sinkhole committee.

Most church committees are not designed to lead change. Many of them are sinkholes. The church or a nominating group of the church selects committee members for a variety of reasons. The reasons, however, are not usually strategic.

Change does not take place if the change coalition does not have credibility with the congregation. Change does not take place if the coalition does not have strategic members. Most church committees are anything but strategic.

They are sinkhole committees.

Who Should Be a Part of the Eager Coalition?

The pastor in the opening story of this chapter took ten months to gather a coalition and meet with them to get their buy-in of the impending change. He was highly strategic in the composition of this group. He did not form a committee or task force, but he made certain the coalition included the right people.

Though all phases of leading change are important, it is this phase where most leaders fail. It takes time and patience, especially in established churches, to build a coalition. And it is vitally important to remember five key descriptors as you seek to form a coalition.

Chemistry. A key word in the description of the coalition is "eager." That means they desire to move forward with the change. They are not perpetual naysayers who seek to derail any idea that is not their own. Though they may not always agree with you at the onset, they are not disagreeable in personality. They have the right chemistry to walk alongside you and others they will influence.

Position. There will be some people who will need to be a part of your eager coalition because they hold key positions in the church. That does not mean every person in every leadership position should be part of the coalition. In one church I served, the treasurer was adversarial to almost anything I tried to lead. I didn't want him as a trusted advisor because, well, I didn't trust him. But I did seek the counsel of other key leaders in the church.

Influence. It does not take a leader long to discover the persons of influence in the church. These influencers may or may not have leadership positions in the congregation, but other members do listen to them. They are the type of people who can turn a church business meeting just by making a few comments. Typically, the influencers do not overuse their sway on others; they are wise and selective.

Expertise. If the desired change in the church involves the church facilities, it would help to have an architect, contractor, or someone knowledgeable in that area. If it involves personnel, it would be good to have someone credible leading people. But a caveat is in order here. You don't seek someone with expertise unless he or she can be an influence on others in the congregation.

Leadership. This descriptor overlaps with some of the others, but it should not be neglected. Those who are true leaders can become outstanding resources to help you lead change. They have been there, and they know what it takes to move forward with significant change.

The Process of Building the Eager Coalition

The process of building an eager coalition is vital to the change leadership, but there is no precise roadmap that describes how you move forward. There are, however, some key lessons we've learned from many change leaders.

First, the process is usually informal. There is no formation of a task force or a committee. The leader typically meets with key persons over a meal, in a coffee shop, or in the office. The leader does indeed present the idea, but the process involves as much listening as it does speaking. And, as change leaders listen, they must be willing to pivot and change as they hear better ideas.

Second, the process is individual. Perhaps there will be times when coalition building involves more than a one-on-one conversation. But they typically work better when the leader gives the person his complete attention. The one-on-one meeting communicates clearly to the church member their importance to the leader.

Third, the process can be lengthy. It may or may not take as long as ten months, but it can seem painfully slow at times. What are some factors that can lengthen the process?

- The greater the level of change, the longer the process of building a coalition takes place.
- The more change-resistant churches obviously require more time than others.

- Typically, shorter-term leaders have to take more time to build a coalition than longer-term leaders.

So, will all your change efforts be as fruitful as the business meeting described at the beginning of this chapter? Probably not. Are you guaranteed to get unanimity if you form the right eager coalition? I doubt it.

But this phase is absolutely vital if you really desire to lead change in your church. Once you get the eager coalition gathered, it's time to formulate and communicate the vision to the rest of the congregation.

To that exciting phase we now turn.

Diagnostic and Study Questions

1. What are some differences between an eager coalition and a sinkhole committee?

2. Describe the differences and similarities between "position" and "influence" as descriptors of the eager coalition.

3. What coalition descriptors fit King Artaxerxes in Nehemiah 2?

4. Look at the three factors that can prolong the coalition building process. Can you provide examples of these in your church?

CHAPTER 6

BECOME A VOICE AND VISION FOR HOPE

I wish I could give millions of church members a glimpse behind the scenes of the lives and ministries of pastors and other church staff. I recently spoke to a pastor who made the transition from a law practice to serving a church with about 225 in attendance. His words were poignant.

"I wish I could have known then what I know now," he began. "When I was practicing law and serving as an elder in the church, I assumed pastors had a pretty sweet job. They got to preach the Word. They had flexible schedules. And it seemed like most people held them in pretty high esteem."

He paused for a moment to gather his thoughts. "I was dead wrong!" he exclaimed. "I never dreamed there were so many critics and nitpickers. I never realized that flexible schedules were really a myth. My wife reminded me we haven't had an uninterrupted vacation since I became a pastor."

He shook his head, somewhat in regret of his lack of awareness in the past. "I had a pretty high pressure corporate law practice," he continued. "I had deadlines, angry clients, and messy litigation. But it pales in comparison to the pressure I feel as a pastor. The only way I can do this job is to be called to it."

Okay, let's look at that last sentence one more time: *The only way I can do this job is to be called to it.*

Hope and Vision

It is exceedingly difficult for pastors and other church leaders to be voices of hope and vision. On the one hand, they are constantly dealing with critics and the tyranny of the urgent with church members. On the other hand, pastors are often emotionally and physically drained from the highs and lows of ministry.

There is a destructive cycle in many congregations. Critics hit the pastor hard. Or the pastor experiences several days of extreme highs and lows in ministry. That leader has no energy left to appear buoyant and hopeful.

Unfortunately, church members often become more demanding and critical when a pastor is down or drained emotionally. I don't see such actions as strategically evil most of the time. Rather, the church members follow the emotions of the pastor's blues, which puts them in a negative mood themselves.

The negativity from church members thus increases. The pastor is thus even more drained and down. And the members feed on that negativity.

You get the picture.

A healthy church has a hopeful and visionary pastor.

The obvious question becomes: How can a pastor or other church leader become hopeful and visionary?

When Vision Leads to Hope

There are many biblical texts speaking powerfully to the truth of hope. Indeed, entire books have been written on hope in the Bible. Here are a selected few texts:

- "I put my hope in you, LORD; You will answer, Lord my God." (Ps. 38:15)
- "Rest in God alone, my soul, for my hope comes from Him." (Ps. 62:5)
- "The LORD values those who fear Him, those who put their faith in His faithful love." (Ps. 147:11)
- "The LORD is my portion; therefore I will put my hope in Him." (Lam. 3:24)
- "And now I stand on trial for the hope of the promise made by God to our fathers." (Acts 26:6)

- "We have also obtained access through Him by faith into this grace in which we stand, and we rejoice in the hope of the glory of God." (Rom. 5:2)
- "Therefore, having such a hope, we use great boldness." (2 Cor. 3:12)
- "Let us hold on to the confession of our hope without wavering, for He who promised is faithful." (Heb. 10:23)

Hope in Christ is a major theological theme of the entirety of Scripture. But sometimes we leaders do not experientially sense that hope. Our faith is there, but our feelings have not followed.

How do we then become instruments of visible hope when we don't feel like it?

I'm glad you asked.

It's Not Cliché: Hope Begins and Continues with God

You picked up this book for a reason. I assume many of you wanted to learn how to become agents of change in your churches.

Here is a simple lesson and beginning point. Change agents are agents of hope. And hope has its being in the heart of God. There is no true hope apart from God.

So . . . what have we learned about leaders of hope?

Leaders who embody hope in their churches have three clearly defined traits:

1. *They read the Bible daily.* This first characteristic seems so simple and basic, and, in a way, it is. But too many leaders do not take time to read the Bible daily. Brad Waggoner, in his book *The Shape of Faith to Come*, presents a fascinating study about spiritual maturity. The essence of the study is that the most mature Christians have one common trait: they read the Bible daily. So it is with leaders as well. You can't have hope if you're not hearing from the Author of hope every day.

2. *They choose to communicate hope.* While there are certainly times to be prophetic, leaders of hope are highly intentional about communicating hope to their congregants. There are always choices in the content and tone of communications. Leaders of hope choose to communicate hope.

3. *They look for low-hanging fruit.* Leaders of hope regularly seek small victories for the church. They likewise seek stories of small victories that take place in the lives of their members and the ministries of the church. We will pursue this topic further in chapter 9.

Pastor Edwin in Kentucky told me he planned to leave his church even though he had no place to go. He was beaten up, despondent, and discouraged. The church members were discouraged as well. To a great extent, they were mirroring the emotions of their pastor.

He began immersing himself in the Bible. It got to be such a habit that he could not imagine a day without reading God's Word. Typically he spent about thirty minutes reading the Bible each day.

He then asked God to give him a hopeful attitude and the ability to communicate God's hope and grace to the church. It was not easy. There were some mean people and vicious critics in the church. The pastor persisted though. And church members began to sense a change in Edwin.

Twice a month the church offered food and clothes to the needy in the community. It was an older ministry in the church faithfully led by only four women and two men, all of them elderly. Most of the church members forgot it existed.

Edwin showed up toward the end of a day where the unnamed ministry had served needy people in the community. He asked one of the leaders how many people they had served that day. To his amazement, the leader showed him the names of 225 people. He also told him they typically served a few more people than that.

The pastor did the math. The church was serving at least 225 people in the community twenty-four times a year, or fifty-four hundred ministry needs met every year.

He shared the numbers with the congregation during a Sunday worship service. The congregation had no idea of the impact of this ministry. They would later learn that twenty-two people had become followers of Christ through this ministry.

Within weeks, donations of clothes, food, and money began to pour into the ministry. More than thirty people asked to be a part of it, including twelve Millennials. The ministry grew rapidly. The church moved from a state of hopelessness to hope.

And the pastor is still serving there—three years later.

The church finally decided to name the ministry. It is called HOPE, helping other people eternally.

Hope Must Accompany Vision

I know. You really want to lead change in your church.

You want to be a part of something that is making a difference.

You want to make a difference.

Some pundits will tell you to create a vision statement and move fast forward. They aren't wrong in their exhortation; they are simply not telling the full story.

Vision is critical to lead change. Vision statements are likewise important in the process. But leaders who shape a vision without a foundation of hope are not doing the church any favors. Such is the reason I shared the hope factor first.

Now let's talk about vision.

It can be a confusing topic. Definitions of "vision" and "mission" abound. On this topic of change, allow me to expand on vision in two ways.

The Guiding Vision: The Discipleship Process

Many years ago, Eric Geiger and I wrote *Simple Church*. The book was based on Eric's research of churches across America. His research found that churches that had a clear process of discipleship were the healthiest by almost any metrics. Eric brilliantly proposed that the vision statement of the church reflect the process of discipleship.

For brevity, allow me to illustrate. Let's suppose that the critical elements of disciple-making at Jordanton Church included: regular attendance in worship services; connecting with a small group; getting involved in a community or international ministry; and giving faithfully to the church.

With those key components of discipleship, Jordanton Church could articulate its vision statement as follows:

Love God. Connect with Others. Serve Others. Give Abundantly.

Thus the vision statement becomes a process of discipleship to move members to regular corporate worship attendance (love God); active involvement in a small group (connect with others); involvement in a local ministry or an overseas mission assignment (serve others); and regular and generous stewardship (give abundantly).

Obviously, there is much more to the simple church model, but at least you get an idea of how a vision statement is used here. I refer to this model as a *guiding vision.* It provides clarity to the expectations of members through a vision statement. And it guides members through an unambiguous process of discipleship.

But for the purpose of change leadership in the church, there is a vision process that is even more powerful. I call this approach the *strategic vision.*

The Strategic Vision: A Specific Plan for a Specific Time

If change leadership is the primary leadership approach the church needs, the strategic vision is best for a season. Here are some of the unique features of the strategic vision:

- It involves a facet of the church's ministry, not all of the church's ministry.
- It typically has specific goals.
- It usually has a specified time frame.
- It is best written as a brief narrative that motivates and encourages.

Here is an example of a strategic vision for Jordanton Church:

Over the next three years, the members of Jordanton Church will be involved in at least three ministries a year to the town of Jordanton. Through these ministries, we will demonstrate our love for the community, our service to the community, and our desire to make Jordanton a better place to live. We will involve at least half of our adult and student members in these expressions of love and ministry.

Can you imagine how the members of the church felt when they embraced this vision statement? They undoubtedly were excited and encouraged about making a difference in their community. They knew they had specific and challenging goals before them. And they became more receptive to change because the members became more concerned about doing ministry rather than the methods that are often the focus points of conflicts.

A Simple Summary

The essence of this facet of change leadership is simple and clear: become a voice of hope and provide a clear vision for the church to move forward in a strategic fashion. Change leaders who provide hope and vision are the most successful change leaders.

It's just that basic.

Diagnostic and Study Questions

1. What are your favorite verses of hope? Why?

2. Why do you see the necessity for the change leader to tie hope to vision?

3. Discuss the three ways a change leader becomes a leader of hope. Why are each of these so critical to the change process?

4. Write a possible strategic vision for your church. Make certain it meets the four descriptors noted in this chapter. If you already have a strategic vision statement, evaluate that statement in light of the four descriptors in this chapter and consider how it may need adjusted or reemphasized.

CHAPTER 7

DEAL WITH PEOPLE ISSUES

 The pastor did not see it coming.

It really wasn't his fault. It's hard to anticipate a staff coup.

The pastor was well loved in the church. He was making changes incrementally, but he definitely was a change agent.

Some of the key changes involved ministry staff. No one was being fired, but ministry responsibilities were being realigned. He was leading, as Jim Collins said in *Good to Great*, by getting the right people in the right seats on the bus.

But a couple of the ministry staff didn't want to change. Instead of sharing their concerns with the pastor, one of the staff took matters into his own hands. He began complaining to a few of the elders about the "dictator pastor." One of those elders was the church bully, a mean-spirited man who always got his way or got mad, real mad.

Those few elders called the pastor to meet with them. Again, the pastor didn't see it coming. They told him they wanted his resignation. The pastor was stunned. They didn't even give him a reason. Though the small group of elders did not have the authority to fire the pastor, he chose to resign anyway. He did not want to put the church through a fight that would have certainly taken place.

No one won.

The pastor resigned.

The pastor and his family were devastated.

Many church members left. They did not understand what had taken place. They were hurt deeply.

The congregation lost over one-third of its attendance. Those who remain are hurt. They don't understand either.

No one won.

Dealing with Reality

So why did I begin this chapter with such a depressing story? My answer is simple: because it reflects reality in many churches.

It would be a sinful disservice to the kingdom and to you if I wrote a book on leading change without addressing some of the painful and dangerous issues that leaders face.

About nine out of ten churches in America have settled into dangerous complacency. Many members have dug in deeply and are headstrong to resist change.

Do not enter into change leadership lightly. Do not begin the process without concerted prayer. And realize that change is all about people. If you don't deal with people issues in leading change, you will fail. It's just that simple.

Though volumes could be written on change and people issues, allow me to provide a succinct guideline for you. I have distilled the topic of people issues and change to seven principles.

1. The Principle of Loving People

If you love change more than you love people, you have already failed as a leader.

You have not been called to your position of leadership to be an organizational despot. You have been called to love and care for people.

Have you ever noticed how much Jesus used the metaphor of sheep and the shepherd? Look at these three examples from John 10.

- "I am the good shepherd. The good shepherd lays down his life for the sheep." (John 10:11)

- "I am the good shepherd. I know My own sheep, and they know me." (John 10:14)
- "My sheep hear my voice, I know them, and they follow Me." (John 10:27)

Leaders are first to care for the sheep. They are to love the sheep. They are to serve the sheep. If change is attempted without love, you have failed already.

But it can get tough. Some of those sheep are unloving. Some of the sheep have messy problems. Some of the sheep are just downright mean!

How do you love all the sheep?

You can't in your own power. That is why change leadership involves an ongoing prayer conversation with God to give you love for all the sheep. He will teach you how to love these sheep.

Don't try it in your own power.

2. The Principle of Expected Opposition

Why do you have to lead change? You lead change because it is not a natural tendency for most people. And if it is not their natural tendency, opposition is the expected reaction.

If you are not being criticized, you are not leading.

Such is the reality of leadership. Such is the reality of change leadership.

I wish I had thicker skin. I admit my envy of some of you leaders who seem impervious to criticism. I have to deal with my thin skin painfully and prayerfully. After six decades, I still get down when someone throws a barb my way.

But if you are a change leader, you will have to deal with critics and opposition.

It is the price leaders have to pay.

3. The Principle of the Eager Coalition

You shouldn't have any doubt about the importance of an eager coalition. I discussed it fully in chapter 5. But let me share a story about a pastor who was able to see the benefits of an eager coalition in a powerful way.

The church, I'll call it Green Hills Church, was relocating. The pastor had done a particularly good job in building a coalition to see the imperative need for a move.

A few days before the proposal was presented to the church as a whole, two of the key leaders took the pastor to lunch. They suggested they assume the role of co-chairpersons for the relocation. They had no desire for power or control; they simply wanted to protect the pastor.

"Pastor," one of the key leaders began, "we are about to make one of the most significant changes in the history of our church. Hundreds of people have been married at this location.

Many loved ones had their funerals here. There are a lot of powerful memories here."

He continued, "No matter how strong a case we make for relocation, there will be pain and grief in the process. Some of that will turn into complaints and questions. We want to protect you from that as much as possible. We will ask people to come to us first with questions and concerns. You need to be leading our church and not be distracted too much."

The two leaders were loved and respected at Green Hills Church. Many members were comfortable going to them with issues rather than the pastor. For sure, there were some who insisted on talking to the pastor. There were some who had to lodge their complaints with the pastor.

But this process helped with the people issue significantly. The eager coalition became an incredible buffer for the pastor.

In less than three years the church had relocated with minimal controversies and loss of members.

4. The Principle of Eating an Elephant

How do you eat an elephant? One bite at a time.

How do you lead a church to change? One careful step at a time.

If you are leading a typical established church to change, many of the members will have gravitated toward change resistance. Such is the nature of an established church. In fact, I tell leaders of these churches to expect members to fall into change categories as follows:

- 5%: Eager for change. This group is wondering what's taking you so long.
- 20%: Open to change. They need to understand the details of the change, but they typically will be okay with it.
- 30%: Followers. They tend to move where the loudest and most convincing voices are.
- 25%: Resistant to change. They like the church just the way it is.
- 20%: Highly resistant to change. This group is not much fun.

While my numbers are not precise, the proportions are close. In most change scenarios, leaders will be fortunate to begin with one-fourth of the congregation on board.

With the rest of the members, you have to move at a pace that can seem painfully slow to a change leader. In fact, nearly half of the members begin with a posture that is resistant to change.

So what is the right pace for change? How do you eat an elephant? I wish I could tell you precisely. Wisdom and discernment are definitely needed here. Keep in mind, though, your sense of a slow pace is usually faster than half the congregation prefers. You will have to deal with each group of members in different, wise, and pastoral ways.

5. The Principle of Not Delaying People Decisions

It was a sunny day in Colorado Springs. The April air still had the feel of winter to it, but the sun gave the illusion of warmth.

I was walking with a pastor named Tommy to talk about some major changes he was anticipating leading in his church.

"One thing I know for sure," he told me somewhat casually, "Brian will not make it on staff."

I paused. Brian was the executive pastor. He had been with Tommy seven years. It was the first time I had heard him articulate this position so clearly. He had made hints about the problem, but nothing this clearly.

We sat on a park bench as I listened to Tommy explain his struggles with Brian. It was definitely a bad chemistry issue, but it also seemed like Brian was not a good fit for his role.

"Let's talk about this," I said. "Brian is a major player in the church. Asking him to step down could be problematic. I've seen leaders lose their jobs when they ask someone to leave."

I offered the option of getting a coach for Brian. "Been there, done that," Tommy responded. "We were clear on our expectations for him, and we told him he was not meeting them."

"What was Brian's response?" I asked. "Nothing," Tommy shrugged. "He did not respond at all. It was almost like he was daring us to do something."

As a second option, I suggested we find him another position in the church. Tommy nixed that idea. It seemed like Brian had burned too many bridges with too many people in the church.

"Wow," I said taking a deep breath. "When will you tell him?"

The pastor's response floored me. "I don't know," he said flatly. "I'm not ready to do anything yet."

Here is the principle: If you know you have to make a difficult decision with someone, don't delay. The situation will only worsen.

But *please* be certain you have no other alternatives.

Otherwise you might be the leader making the exit.

6. The Principle of Losses

The young man was part of a group of pastors I was mentoring. He had led his church to move from one site to three in just two years. The new sites were formerly dying churches that had requested the merger.

Hardly any of the members were familiar with the concept of a multisite church, but the pastor did a masterful job of leading the congregation into these new areas.

So I was surprised when, in a phone conversation, he told me he was really down about the changes. He got right to the point, "We lost three families."

I wanted to laugh, but that would not have been very pastoral. The church had more than five hundred attendees every Sunday, and they lost "only" three families in the course of major changes. I was actually surprised at the low number of exiting members.

But those three families were members he loved. They were people he had counted on to lead the church in this new phase of ministry. It broke his heart that they left because of the changes.

Pastors and other church leaders typically grieve when some members can't make the changes. But it is another painful price of change leadership.

You simply have to expect some membership losses.

7. The Principle of Ongoing Prayer

Please don't forget how leading change begins. Go back to chapter 3 if you need to look at it. Change begins in the power and strength of God.

Leading change begins with prayer.

This principle is especially powerful as you lead people toward change. Leaders are prone to move in their own strength and power. Leaders are action oriented. They often don't take time to pause and pray.

Pray for the entire congregation. Pray for the eager coalition. And pray for those who oppose you and criticize you. Pray *with* them as well.

Sharon was the pastor's fiercest critic. You could be assured she would stand up in a business meeting to oppose anything Pastor Nathan suggested.

When Nathan began to lead the church in a major building endeavor, Sharon had a litany of complaints to unload on him. And so she did . . . right after the worship service.

The pastor invited Sharon away from the crowd to a counseling room. He let her detail every concern and criticism she had. Thirty or more minutes passed. Nathan remained quiet.

When Sharon ended her rant, Nathan simply asked for a time of prayer. He prayed that God would show him where he was wrong. He prayed for corrections in his own leadership. He prayed sincere prayers of praise for the strengths she offered.

He was never defensive, only prayerful. Sharon left the room. She was quiet for the first time.

The change in Sharon was not overnight, but it was rather quick. Within six months, Sharon became one of Nathan's biggest supporters.

Do all stories of opposition and critics end this way? No.

But I do know prayer is powerful and purposeful. Prayer should be the centerpiece of our lives as we lead people toward change.

As leaders, we do not want to change people. We want God to change people.

And that includes us leaders as well.

Diagnostic and Study Questions

1. Read John 10. Explain Jesus' relationship to the sheep. Why do you think he used this metaphor?

2. How should a leader deal with opposition and critics when leading change?

3. What are some of the reasons people leave churches during major change? How should we respond?

4. Compare the percentages of change receptivity in this chapter to your best guess of the percentages for your own church. What do the differences tell you?

CHAPTER 8

MOVE FROM AN INWARD FOCUS TO AN OUTWARD FOCUS

 I respectfully request a closed casket at my funeral.

Yes, I'm an introvert. But my introversion should not be a factor when I'm dead.

I'm peculiar in this respect, but I simply don't want people looking at my body and saying, "He looks so natural."

What does that mean? I think it's just another way of saying, "He looks so dead."

Please close the casket. I don't want to look natural.

You see, the natural progression of men and women is to move toward death. That has been our fate ever since the Fall. The cross of Christ provided a supernatural means of grace to eternal life.

But death is the natural path, both for humanity and for churches.

Here's how it usually goes with churches. A church begins with a desire to reach its community. The effort of the congregation is disproportionally outward. There is an urgency to get the message of the gospel and the new church to those in the area.

Over time, the efforts of the church typically begin to move inwardly. Most of the ministry is for the members. Most of the activities are for the members. Most of the financial resources are for the members. Most of the leadership's time is for the members.

Within five years, the church has moved 90 percent inwardly by almost any metric. The church, just a few years earlier, proclaimed the Great Commission. Now it's focused on the great comfort.

Many churches move from a dynamic Great Commission body to a religious country club. The members pay their "dues," and you better make certain they are happy and well served.

Give them the programs they want. Give them the music style they want. Give them the color of the carpet they want. Give them the sermon length they want. Give them the best parking spots. And don't dare sit in "their" pews or chairs.

The local congregation moved from being all about him to being all about them.

Me. Myself. And I.

That's the natural state of most churches in America today. They have become inwardly focused and self-serving. Business meetings are often battles to be fought rather than God's business.

And now you desire to lead this church to change?

If you followed any of the sequence of this book, you have taken some major steps. You have taken time to pray, to seek God's strength and wisdom in leading change. You have confronted realities and communicated a sense of urgency. You have begun to build an eager coalition. You have even begun to communicate a message of hope and vision. And you have begun to deal with some of the people issues.

But change will not happen without intentional outward movement. Allow me to explain.

All of the facets of change leadership to this point have been about "being" and "saying." Little has been done about "doing." Simply stated, your church will not likely be ready for change until it experiences some action steps of an outward focus.

This outward focus prepares the members for change. It gets them looking beyond their own needs to the needs of their community and the world.

It's analogous to an obese person seeking to change his health and weight. He can read all the great health and diet books. He can have people to whom he is accountable. He can have a great attitude.

But until he actually starts exercising and eating a proper diet, he will remain obese. He has to take those first steps. And those first steps are preparatory for the ultimate desired change: a truly healthy body.

In the next two chapters, I will share how leaders can help a congregation take these first action steps. The idea is to move from the natural state of an inwardly focused organization to the supernatural state of an outwardly focused organization.

Let's look at four action items for churches to move outwardly.

The Outwardly-Focused Leader

Do you really want to lead change in your church? If so, you have to be a clear example for change yourself. Whether you are a pastor, elder, staff person, or lay leader, you can't lead change without embodying change.

Let me give you a clear example.

I was leading a coaching group of twelve church leaders, eight of whom were lead pastors. All of them were in churches that were inwardly focused. I gave the group one external assignment. I asked them to be intentional each week about inviting someone to church or sharing the gospel of Christ with them. They were to be accountable to me via a brief e-mail each week.

The results surprised me, really surprised me. At the end of one year, ten of the twelve churches had begun to grow. All of the eight churches where the pastor made the commitment were growing.

Did you get that?

God used one person, a key leader, in ten churches, to be his instrument for revitalization.

Turnaround begins with you.

Outward focus begins with you.

Revitalization begins with you.

Or allow me to be biblically precise. In each of these churches God used one person as his instrument for turnaround.

What can you do as a leader to become more outwardly focused in your church? Are you willing to be accountable to someone for that Great Commission behavior?

Many times change leadership is just that basic.

The Outwardly-Focused Budget

It is amazing what two hours can do to move a church in a new direction.

Cliff, the executive pastor, met with Jon, the lead pastor about a conviction he had.

"Look," Cliff began. "We have been talking a lot about what we need to do to lead the church in a Great Commission focus. None of us are happy with the stagnant trends we are experiencing."

The executive pastor continued, "I am the staff member responsible for our budget. I have the same conviction that you do about leading our church outwardly. But I think we have a real problem inherent in our budget."

He had Jon's attention now. "What are you talking about?" Jon asked with anticipation.

Cliff showed Jon a brief document he had put together. "Our total budget, "Cliff reminded him, "is $1.1 million." Jon nodded affirmatively. "But do you see these nine other numbers?" Cliff asked rhetorically. "They represent different parts of the budget where we are subsidizing trips for church members. The total is $120,000, more than 10 percent of our budget!"

"What?" Jon exclaimed. He rubbed his eyes as if he were seeing things that were not really there.

"That's exactly my reaction," Cliff responded. "We are a middle class church where most, if not all, of our members can pay their on way. But we have created a subsidy and entitlement mentality in our budget. The numbers have been hidden in nine different line items."

Now the pastor was under conviction too. The church had become so inwardly focused that one of the major expenses were subsidies for members who did not need subsidies.

Jon and Cliff presented these findings to the finance committee and elders. They too were stunned and ready to change things immediately. But one of the older and wiser elders suggested they move in a slightly different direction.

"Look, we have our quarterly business meeting coming up in two weeks," he said. "Instead of coming into a meeting with plans to slash and cut, let's have a town hall type meeting where we present the facts, but then get ideas how we could use those funds toward the Great Commission."

There was unanimity of spirit, so they moved forward.

The quarterly business meeting, now called a town hall, had an air of excitement and anticipation. Church members were asked ahead of time to think about ways the church could better serve and connect with the community.

The chairman of the finance committee showed the subsidy amount, but immediately asked this question: "What could we do with these funds to reach our community?"

Some of the longer-term members said it was the best business meeting they could remember. For two hours, the members dreamed and ultimately came to a consensus about how the funds would be used. No one complained at all about the subsidies going away. A couple of members did ask how the church ever got to this point, but they moved on shortly thereafter.

The church's budget became outwardly focused. A new energy was obvious in the church.

A point of this story is certainly to share how one church became more outwardly focused with its budget. But the greater point is to articulate that the church would soon make some major changes. And no one believed those changes would have been possible without some evidence of moving toward an outward focus.

And it was accomplished in a business meeting in only two hours.

Outwardly Focused in Increments

We've all heard the cliché, "People won't change unless they want to change."

It's similar with churches. Change usually does not take place until church members see positive evidence that it is good for the church. Such is the purpose of this step in leading change. When a church is becoming outwardly focused, it is certainly changing. But it is also preparatory for even greater change that can be introduced later.

At this point, the effort should be on incrementally becoming more outwardly focused.

Leaders can do something incrementally to become outwardly focused.

A small group can volunteer to do something in the community that's never been done.

The elders can make a commitment to do one small thing to become outwardly focused.

You get the picture.

You are leading incremental change to prepare the church for greater change.

Outwardly Focused and Low-Hanging Fruit

In his seminal work on change leadership in the secular world, *Leading Change,* John Kotter talks about "generating short-term wins." He sees this as a crucial step in leading an organization toward major change.

My thoughts are similar, but I prefer to use the metaphor of "low-hanging fruit." It seems to paint a vivid picture of potential reality. The idea is to demonstrate from an incremental perspective how the impending change will be a positive outcome for the church. The leader seeks to find and articulate easier victories for the church that will lead to greater and potentially, more challenging, victories.

When I served as a pastor in St. Petersburg, Florida, we had an orange tree in our front yard. The tree was not that tall, but neither am I. On several occasions in season, I would go outside and pick an orange off the tree. Of course, I would always pick the low-hanging fruit, because it was the easiest to get.

Think about the major change or changes your church needs to make. What low-hanging fruit can you find that is a step toward those changes?

We have been looking at incremental changes that are not necessarily connected to the goal of the desired greater change. The purpose of finding low-hanging fruit is to make a first step toward that desired change.

At the risk of stepping on toes, let me offer an example. Hear me clearly. My purpose is not to be either an advocate or opponent of Sunday evening services. It is, however, a change issue that crosses my desk frequently. A church whose Sunday morning worship attendance was six hundred had a Sunday evening worship attendance of seventy. It was clearly something the church as a whole did not want to continue.

The major change the leadership desired was eliminating the Sunday evening worship service. But about two hundred people were vociferously opposed to the move. Of course, that meant a number of people who were opposed never attended the service. But that's another topic.

The leadership of the church found low-hanging fruit. The attendance of the Sunday evening attendance drops to thirty in the summer. The leadership suggested they "take a break" from Sunday evening services for ten weeks in the summer. The idea was embraced by most of the members.

One year later the leadership was able to eliminate the services year round.

This step of finding low-hanging fruit thus becomes a clear stepping-stone to even more substantive change. In fact, it's such an important issue that we will take time to delve into it more fully in the next chapter.

Diagnostic and Study Questions

1. Why do most churches become inwardly focused?

2. Give some clear examples of outwardly-focused leaders in the New Testament.

3. What is the biggest difference between finding low-hanging fruit and other incremental moves toward an outward focus?

4. Do you know what components of your church's budget are outwardly focused?

CHAPTER 9

PICK LOW-HANGING FRUIT

 "We've never done it that way before."

"That doesn't work at our church."

"The people in the community won't respond to us."

The story is true. I have modified some elements to preserve the anonymity of the pastor, but this story is based on real facts, real numbers, and real people.

The issue is common. The church was inwardly focused. The solutions were lacking. Even more tragic than the dearth of solutions was a congregation that was apathetic, disillusioned, and distrusting.

The leadership of the church had a bold vision. The church of three hundred in worship attendance would invite to church three thousand unchurched in the community in three months. The vision was simply called "3 x 3 x 3." Every church member was encouraged to invite at least ten people during those three months. They would report their invitations digitally, and the church website would keep track of the total.

But Pastor Greg sensed the apathy. The vision was bold, but the apathy was greater. And he began to hear the excuses articulated above. He knew this vision would fail if some change did not take place.

Greg told the congregation he wanted their permission to do something smaller as a trial run. It was his version of low-hanging fruit. He called it "Invite Your One."

Instead of a massive invasion of the community, they would ask every member to invite at least one person to church on a specific Sunday. They would have about a four-week build-up time, where each member shared the name of the person they invited. The cumulative number of invitations would be posted on the website.

Friendly contests were suggested. For example, the adult small groups pastor challenged each group to have the greatest number invited.

On the initial Sunday of the build-up, the pastor, elders, and staff shared the names of their invited guests. There was a palpable excitement when Greg shared the name of his guest: the mayor of the city.

It was really a simple concept. Everyone invite at least one person for a specific worship service. For Greg and the leadership, Invite Your One was low-hanging fruit. The commitment expected of the members was low: invite one person to church.

The buy-in was much better than the massive 3 x 3 x 3. And though the leadership still had detractors, doubters, and discouragers, Invite Your One proved to be a great success.

The church's worship attendance increased over 50 percent on that day, from 300 to 465. And though the number settled to around 360 in subsequent Sundays, average worship attendance was still up 20 percent.

Beyond the numerical growth, something even more importantly began to take place among the members. They experienced positive responses when they invited people. They previously believed the myth that no one would come to the services if they invited them.

The congregation was moving from an inward focus to an outward focus. Momentum was in place. Doubters had been convinced or sidelined.

The church was now ready for more significant change.

In any successful change effort of low-hanging fruit, three elements must be present. The leadership of the church did a great job of making certain all three elements were there:

1. Visibility
2. Clear results
3. Clearly related to the major change initiative

Characteristic #1: Visibility

Low-hanging fruit is a test run or an introduction to a major change. When I was twelve years old, I told my mom I wanted to play trumpet in the middle school band. Mom knew two things about me. First, I preferred to spend my extracurricular time in competitive athletics. Second, I had no musical ability.

Instead of buying a trumpet, she rented one. Mom did not tell me at the time lest I become discouraged with her lack of faith in my ability.

I quit trumpet lessons after three weeks.

It's really okay for low-hanging fruit to fail. It means the trial run did not work, but the church did not invest the resources in a major endeavor.

Successful low-hanging fruit efforts are evident to almost everyone in the church. At the very least, there is a sense of encouragement in the congregation that something went well. Typically, though, the evidence is so compelling that the church becomes highly enthused. The excitement is palpable.

When Greg's congregation initiated Invite Your One, the effort was clearly visible to everyone in the church. The trial run or low-hanging fruit began with efforts by the leadership, but it soon became a church-wide effort embraced by many.

Characteristic #2: Clear Results

Attendance increased over 50 percent on the culmination day of Invite Your One. Attendance remained 20 percent higher from that point forward. The church saw the one-day impact of the effort, and the congregants saw the sustained impact of Invite Your One.

No one could challenge the results of the efforts. They might object to the approach or to the type of emphasis, but they could not doubt the results.

Successful low-hanging fruit results will be clear, compelling, and, potentially, paradigm shifting.

Characteristic #3: Clearly Related to the Major Change Initiative

The church leaders did not see Invite Your One as the answer to all the problems for needed change in the congregation. They viewed it as low-hanging fruit that could lead to greater and closely related change.

In the previous chapter we looked at the stage of leading the church to an outward focus. We offered suggestions and ideas to guide that effort.

The stage of outward focus is wide open to a plethora of directions. Any biblically sound approach should be on the table.

While the stage of picking low-hanging fruit is indeed a means to help the church move to an outward focus, this stage has to have a greater purpose. The success of the low-hanging fruit must point to a greater desired change. Of course, the greater change in the church with Invite Your One was to create a new ethos and culture of inviting people.

Clearly, Invite Your One was a successful venture in low-hanging fruit. It was highly visible to the church. It demonstrated clear results. And it was tied closely to the greater change effort of creating a culture that invites people to church.

Picking low-hanging fruit is not simply something that helps the change process. It is a vital and necessary stage of the change process. Among others, there are six key reasons this stage is so valuable.

The Role and Value of Picking Low-Hanging Fruit

Lest the change leader in any church doubt the value of picking low-hanging fruit, look at what this stage can accomplish:

1.   Demonstrates the effort was worth it
2.   Affirms change leaders
3.   Clarifies strategies and tactics
4.   Overcomes resistance
5.   Builds momentum toward the greater change

Demonstrates the Effort Was Worth It

I have not addressed failure with picking low-hanging fruit, but it needs to be mentioned. After all, not every effort at this stage will succeed. Most will, but some won't.

The stage of low-hanging fruit will accomplish a goal regardless of its success or failure. If it is a failure, you can remind others that the purpose of the stage was to attempt a trial run. Not all trial runs are successful. And their failures are not nearly as painful as more significant and widespread changes are.

But, in the likely event the low-hanging fruit stage is successful, leaders have immediate confirmation the effort was worth it. Indeed, if there is any singular benefit of this stage, it is the confirmation of the effort.

Affirms Change Leaders

Most change leaders have their own fear and trepidation. Courage is not the absence of fear; it is the will to move forward despite the fear. Change leaders have their own doubts despite an external bravado visible to others.

When the stage of low-hanging fruit demonstrates success, change leaders are encouraged and motivated. They are affirmed in their courageous decision. They have a motivation to continue the process. They no longer question if they should move forward. They are encouraged to continue their tenure at the church.

I have seen change leaders skip this stage and move directly to the more pervasive and substantive change. Unfortunately, I have seen many of those same leaders become discouraged, disillusioned, and even dismissed because the church could not handle the change.

If I could see you face-to-face or have a chat with you over the phone, I would urge you, even beg you, to pick low-hanging fruit. I truly believe you will experience an incredible affirmation of your leadership.

Clarifies Strategies and Tactics

I love to read Proverbs. One of these days, I will commit about sixty days to reading each Proverb slowly and thoughtfully. The Proverbs are filled with practical wisdom on planning, strategies, and tactics. For example, Proverbs 15:22 says: "Plans fail when there is no counsel, but with many advisers they succeed."

Here is another great contribution of the low-hanging fruit. You and many other people get to see what is working or not working on a relatively small scale. With this collective insight and wisdom, you are able to proceed more wisely with the larger change later.

You get greater clarity on your plans, strategies, and tactics. It is a priceless opportunity to get it right.

Overcomes Resistance

One of the biggest benefits of the low-hanging fruits effort is to show the naysayers that it can be done. Here is a profile of the typical established church membership related to change receptivity from an earlier chapter. I have simply added the name "adopters" for clarity.

- Eager early adopters: 5%
- Willing adopters: 20%
- Crowd-following adopters: 30%
- Resistant adopters: 25%
- Highly resistant adopters: 20%

A leader in a church typically begins with about one-fourth of the congregation ready to attempt changes. They are the eager early adopters and willing adopters.

About 30 percent of the congregation will basically go the direction they sense the church is moving. They desire to join the crowd regardless of the decisions.

But 45 percent of the congregation begins at some level of resistance. Their default response is "no."

Most ventures in low-hanging fruit move the crowd-following adopters (30%) to becoming genuine adopters. And it is not unusual for a majority of the resistant adopters to switch positions.

In this example, only 25 percent of the congregation was on board before the low-hanging fruit effort. But about 70 percent were ready to move forward after the effort.

Moving from 25 percent to 70 percent: It's a no-brainer.

Builds Momentum for the Greater Change

At the risk of redundancy, let me remind you that picking low-hanging fruit is a clear and, usually, necessary step for moving forward with the major change. To be certain, I have seen a number of cases where major change was implemented without the trial run of the low-hanging fruit.

Some of the exceptions included:

- The change leader had long tenure and had led in a major change in the past.
- The church has an urgent need that cannot wait for the trial run of picking low-hanging fruit.
- The church was desperate, sometimes close to death.
- The type of change to be implemented had already been accomplished in some churches known to many of the members.

Most of the time, however, this stage is not only important, it is vital. It is both the first step toward the major change, as well as a builder of momentum toward that change. Failure to demonstrate on a smaller scale that such a venture can work often means failure for the entire change initiative.

Too many church leaders have spoken with me after a failed change effort wondering where they could have possibly gone wrong. Often I learn they plunged into the depths of the major change without putting their toes in the water of the smaller change.

Be patient. The efforts you make toward picking low-hanging fruit will prove well worth the work and time.

Diagnostic and Study Questions

1. Explain how the example of Invite Your One worked as a low-hanging fruit.

2. What are some major changes needed in your church? What could be some low-hanging fruit to move in that direction?

3. Look in the book of Proverbs and find three verses dealing with planning or change. Note how they related to change in the church. 15 ; 22, 16: 3

4. What are some possibilities where the stage of picking low-hanging fruit should be skipped? Do any of those possibilities exist in your church?

CHAPTER 10

IMPLEMENT AND CONSOLIDATE CHANGE

If there was a textbook on leading change in the church, Ryan's change leadership was it.

The Donnard Community Church was not located in Donnard anymore. In fact, the community of Donnard no longer existed. But the church continued to exist with the same name in a rapidly declining no-name community.

Almost every parcel of land near and around the church had been zoned industrial. There were no homes near the church. Indeed, the church facility looked completely out-of-place in the midst of the warehouses and manufacturing buildings.

Ryan took his time leading the church to change. He had been pastor for four years before he began suggesting the church relocate and change its name. He knew and loved the members. And he knew many of them would resist any significant change.

He led the stage of picking the low-hanging fruit well. The church leased a facility for one service a month for six months in the community where they would eventually move. The members became accustomed to the new community. They learned the best routes to drive there.

Donnard Community Church sold for almost 40 percent more than anyone expected. Two companies on each side of the church desired the property, and they got into a bidding war. The church had sufficient funds to buy property and build a facility debt free.

Three years passed. The relocation was successful. No members dropped out of the church. There was excitement and near unanimity of positive reactions to the new building.

The new church took the name of the community where it was now located. Donnard Community Church became Frank's Creek Community Church. The inaugural worship event was the best event anyone in the church could remember.

The church's enthusiastic spirit became a draw for residents in the community. For the first time in twenty-three years, the church was growing.

It seemed to be a classic case of change leadership done well. Sure, there were a few bumps, but the entire process was a grand case study.

But, fifteen months after relocation, Pastor Ryan resigned. No one, absolutely no one, saw it coming. He simply said he was burned out.

The church began to decline again shortly after his departure.

Getting the Vision and Low-Hanging Fruit Right

Methodologically, Ryan and the church leadership did everything right. Give credit to one of the wise deacons for coming up with the idea of holding monthly worship services in the prospective community. It was the perfect low-hanging fruit to lead to the greater change of relocation.

But, if you could hear the subtlety of the communication during the phase of low-hanging fruit, you would have noticed problems forming early. For example, the unofficial but often spoken vision of the church was to see if Frank's Creek was a community of choice for the church.

Indeed, once the church voted to sell and relocate, the vision was explicit: "Creating a New History in a New Community."

Do you see the subtle problem that became a larger problem? From the stage of the low-hanging fruit to the totality of relocation, the vision was about moving to a new place.

The problem with such a vision is that it has no sustaining power. Once the move is complete, nothing is left to accomplish. A better vision statement would be: "Becoming a Church with a Passion to Minister and Reach Our Community." With that vision, the work is just beginning at the point of relocation.

Pastor Ryan fell to the same danger. He made his ministry all about the relocation. It should have been about leading the church to more effective Great Commission ministry, but that was not the case.

So when the relocation was complete, Ryan felt despondent and low on energy. He no longer had a guiding vision to lead the church. The vision was complete. Done. Over.

Indeed, a misstated vision can become a major downfall for a church in the midst of change. Most of the misstated visions are like Ryan's church's vision; the means became the end.

Let's look at five keys for implementing and consolidating the change initiatives:

1. The power of over-communicating
2. The power of transparency
3. Dealing with dissenters
4. Dealing with success
5. Dealing with complacency

The Power of Over-Communicating

Presuming the vision is on target at the onset, how much should leaders communicate the vision and the change needed to fulfill the vision? As a rule of thumb, once leaders are sick and tired of hearing themselves say the same thing over and over again, that is the beginning point of effective communication.

Simply stated, I have never seen or heard a major change initiative and its accompanying vision repeated too much. Leaders often get bored with their redundancy. But it is absolutely necessary for the congregation as a whole. They must be reminded again and again.

Obviously, communicating the vision and the elements of the change process in the midst of the change is important. But it is equally important to keep the vision before the congregation after specific changes are complete. Change is not true change until it is ingrained in the culture.

Watch the behavioral patterns of the church members. See if they have incorporated the changes in their own lives. See if resistance is still significant. Once members stop talking about the changes as changes, you can be certain those changes are ingrained in the culture.

That takes time, often a lot of time.

Keep communicating.

The Power of Transparency

Great leaders are transparent leaders. Great change takes place when the leaders are transparent.

If there is any sense among the members of the church that information is being withheld, the change process is already in danger. We live in the internet age of transparency. Information is at our fingertips. Everyone expects to be fully informed. Change can be hijacked in a few days if there is any sense of the leadership lacking full disclosure.

Though disclosure is vital for all generations, it is especially important to the Millennial generation. Those young adults, born between 1980 and 2000, are very sensitive to the matter of transparency. If you are open and forthright with them, they will be with you for the change process. If not, they will bail immediately.

Dealing with Dissenters

Let's return to the story of Donnard Community Church and its relocation and renaming to Frank's Creek Community Church. When the day of moving and worship celebration about all the changes took place, there was one group who was as celebratory as anyone else. They were the original dissenters to the relocation.

Why would they be celebrating something they opposed? The dissenters were celebrating *closure* of change, not the change itself. They felt they had survived the ordeal and were now ready to get back to their world of constancy and consistency. For them, the change was over.

The dissenters want the urgency to end and complacency to resume. Though they would never articulate in such a way, they are truly change averse. They are ready to resume their dissent if there are signs that the change is not complete.

But change is never complete. The urgency can never end.

Dealing with Success

It's not just the dissenters who can fall prey to the sense of completion. It is the rest of the congregation and even the leaders. That is what took place at Frank's Creek Community Church. They expended huge amounts of energy and resources toward relocation. They had an incredible service to celebrate the move.

And then it was over.

The congregation and the leaders measured success by a singular event. But true biblical success is ongoing faithfulness.

The critics celebrated the success, and they were poised to oppose any further change.

The pastor celebrated the success, and he entered into a period of despondency and listlessness. He did not stay long after the relocation. He did not have a vision beyond the relocation, so he had no desire to lead the church further.

The entire congregation had a sense of arrival. Again, they saw the relocation as the end instead of the means. And when the end is achieved, there is nothing left to do. That is why one of the greatest challenges for a church that has successfully completed change is to enter into a period of complacency.

Dealing with Complacency

The most frequent congregational responses to successful change is complacency. Part of the complacency comes from the intense pace inherent in major change. Like most organizations, churches often depend on relatively few leaders during such periods of change.

They are worn out. They need a break. They deserve a break.

But breaks can become extended periods of inactivity. From there complacency gives birth.

Getting a re-start can be difficult. Many in modes of complacency remain there. Such is the price at times for successful change.

But the number one reason for complacency is the failure to have a clear vision. As I noted earlier with Frank's Creek Community Church, the stated and repeated vision was relocation. So when the relocation was complete, change efforts ceased. Complacency became normative among church members, only to be exacerbated when the pastor resigned.

When should church leaders deal with the issue of complacency? The answer is not always received well, but church leaders must *always* deal with this issue. It is an ever-present and lurking danger.

So what are the best paths church leaders should take? If there is one theme that must be ever present, it is the theme of urgency.

Keeping It Urgent

Churches should never have periods lacking urgency. We have the most important message to give to the world. The gospel is the only way of salvation. Millions upon millions need to hear the message. The local church is one of God's key instruments for sharing the Word and love of the gospel.

We don't have the luxury of not keeping it urgent.

Most churches today are not urgent. And most American churches today are declining and even dying.

Several years ago, I wrote a book about what a biblical local congregation should look like. I thank God the book, *I Am a Church Member*, has sold more than a million copies. And my sense of praise is not for the sales per se. It is for the potential mind-sets that have been changed among church members.

The book was about selflessness among church members. It was about a serving spirit. It was about all church members becoming contributing and functioning church members as Paul describes in 1 Corinthians 12.

It was about urgency.

In too many of our churches, we act like it is a religious country club. We pay our dues and expect to be served. It is little wonder we fight and argue about petty matters while eternity hangs in the balance for so many. As long as church is about me, myself, and I, we will never have a sense of urgency.

Change is not the end. It is the means. It is the process. Urgency, therefore, precedes change, accompanies change, and leads change again.

At any point the urgency in the church ceases, change ceases, and the church is no longer the church. A true Great

Commission church is always urgent about making disciples. Church members with a sense of urgency are like Peter and John, standing before the Sanhedrin with their freedom and lives on the line, who said "for we are unable to stop speaking about what we have seen and heard" (Acts 4:20).

Change is a process. Throughout the process of healthy change is the sense of urgency.

Our message is one of eternal importance. We don't lead change for change sake. We lead change for the sake of the gospel.

Change is urgent because the gospel is urgent.

It is just that basic.

Diagnostic and Study Questions

1. Why do church members resist needed and necessary change?

2. Explain how success can be an impediment to further change in the church.

3. Read 1 Corinthians 12. Describe a biblical church member from that chapter. How does it differ from most church members today?

4. Explain how the Great Commission of Matthew 28:18–20 should be a call to urgency in most churches. How does Acts 1:8 communicate a sense of urgency?

CHAPTER 11

LIFE IS SHORT. MAKE A DIFFERENCE.

It is a sin to be good when God has called us to be great.

We do not refer to Matthew 28:18–20 as the *Good* Commission. It is the *Great* Commission.

Nor do we read Matthew 22:37–40 and say we just read the *Good* Commandment. It is the *Great* Commandment.

And when Paul wrote the magnificent 13th chapter of 1 Corinthians, he did not say love was one of the *good* things. He said it was the *greatest* of these.

I hope you get my point.

When we read in Scripture those things that are really important, the Bible speaks of them in superlative terms, like "great" or "greatest."

Do you think God wants you to lead your church as a good leader or a great leader?

I know. It's a silly if not rhetorical question. God wants us to be the best stewards we can possibly be. Read the parable of the talents in Matthew 25:14–30 or Luke 19:12–28 again if you have any doubts.

Lives not fully lived are the worst kinds of stewardship.

I presume you who are reading this book are church leaders. You are a pastor. A church staff member. An elder. A deacon. A key lay leader.

God has given you a local congregation to steward. You have been given the talents. Will you use them wisely or bury them in fear or desire for comfort?

I could provide you a plethora of data and statistics on the state of American congregations. It's not a pretty picture.

We are reaching fewer people. Our backdoors are open widely. Church conflict is normative. Pastors and church staff are wounded. Many have given up altogether.

Of course, there are exceptions to the dire description I just provided. That's the problem. They are exceptions.

Most of our congregations need to change. Many of our congregations are on life support and need immediate change. The great need in our churches is for change leaders who are willing to make a difference.

The cost and the risks can be scary. But it wouldn't be called faith if we could tackle these challenges in our own strength and power.

It is a sin to be good when God has called us to be great.

We need change leaders in our churches who are willing to do something great.

The Process of Leading Change

Let's be reminded of the process of change in churches. How do you eat an elephant? One bite at time. Reviewing each of these stages of change is a good reminder that the process takes place one bite at a time.

Stop and Pray

The crucial foundational issue often
neglected in leading change

Confront and Communicate a Sense of Urgency

Facing and sharing the bru-
tal facts with the congregation

Build an Eager Coalition

Most churches have at least a few members ready to move forward.

Become a Voice and Vision of Hope

Members look to leaders for hope and possibilities

Deal with People Issues

The courage to handle people blockage, both staff and church members

Move from an Inward Focus to an Outward Focus

Steadily moving the church beyond
mostly focusing on herself

Pick Low-Hanging Fruit

Clear victories are necessary to sustain positive momentum.

Implement and Consolidate Change

Gospel urgency never ends.
Complacency is always a danger.

Take Time to Pray

Hear me clearly. Deciding to shortcut this stage is a decision to fail. Sure, prayer takes time. And it could seem to be a lot quicker process if you went straight to action. But leading change in the church can only work if it is God-led, God-powered, and God-ordained.

In the earlier statement on greatness, I referred to the Great Commission. We often associate the Great Commission with Matthew 28:19–20: "Go, therefore, and make disciples of all nations, baptizing them in the name of the Father and of the Son and of the Holy Spirit, teaching them to observe everything I have commanded you. And remember, I am with you always, to the end of the age."

Those verses certainly are the verses of the Great Commission, but they are not all of them, even in the Gospel of Matthew. We often dissociate the preceding verse, but it is vital to the Great Commission: "Then Jesus came near and said to them, 'All authority has been given to Me in heaven and on earth'" (Matt. 28:18).

Did you get that? Before you go to make disciples, you remember where your authority derives. Jesus makes it clear it comes from him. We should be clear that we are dependent on him in all things, including leading change.

Take time to pray before and while leading change.

The Sense of Urgency

If church members do not see the vital need in doing things differently, they will be totally change resistant. Glen Marvell was particularly good at communicating urgency during a worship service.

The pastor had been pleading with the church members to embrace a vision for reaching more young families. His pleas had fallen on deaf ears.

But on one Sunday morning, he asked the congregants if they had any children or grandchildren who were not churchgoers. When he saw several nods, he went further. He asked those who had unchurched children and grandchildren to stand so that the church could pray for them.

It was amazing. The church members were blown away. Over 80 percent of the attendees were standing. After a time of prayer, Pastor Glen looked over the congregation and said softly but forcibly, "Do you have any doubt now why we have to reach young families?"

They got the point. They got the urgency.

Finding a Coalition

Leaders who attempt to lead change do not lead change alone.

Take time to find that group of leaders who will charge the hill with you in leading this change.

The book of Proverbs reminds us repeatedly to find others to help us accomplish our plans: "Without guidance, people fall, but with many counselors there is deliverance" (Prov. 11:14). In a similar vein: "Plans fail when there is no counsel, but with many advisers they succeed" (Prov. 15:22).

Lead change with an eager coalition.

Vision and Hope

Leading change means you provide a clear path where the church needs to go. Church members want to be a part of something that makes a difference. And they want to make a difference themselves.

But it is not just the path or the vision they need. They need to hear from leaders how God will lead them to this new point. They need to hear hope.

Vision and hope create a powerful tandem toward leading change in the church.

The People Challenge

The most effective church leaders first love the members of the church. It's not always easy with some of the criticisms and nay-saying that's out there.

In chapter 7, I shared the change receptivity of a typical body of church members. The numbers are telling:

- 5%: Eager for change. This group is wondering what's taking you so long.
- 20%: Open to change. They need to understand the details of the change, but they typically will be okay with it.
- 30%: Followers. They tend to move where the loudest and most convincing voices are.
- 25%: Resistant to change. They like the church just the way it is.
- 20%: Highly resistant to change. This group is not much fun.

In leading change in a church, you are typically dealing with three major groups: those open to change; those who follow others; and those who are resistant to change.

It's not easy. But it is critical you understand you are not dealing with uniformity when you are leading change.

And you must love all the people.

Moving Outwardly

One of the key reasons church members are resistant to change is their inward focus. Unfortunately, many of our congregations have become religious country clubs where the primary purpose is to meet the members' every whim and desire.

Change leaders in churches recognize that the congregation is not ready for change in their present inwardly focused state. They take beginning steps to move the church to a greater outward focus.

Low-Hanging Fruit

The concept of low-hanging fruit in leading change is simple. Demonstrate to the congregation that bigger change is possible by leading in smaller change toward the same goal.

Leaders in a church in Florida desired to make a major impact in their community by "adopting" a nearby public elementary school. The church and its members would make themselves available year round for any service the school needed.

Church members initially balked at the idea of being available for service on a year-round basis. They didn't know what the details of the commitment would be, and they didn't know if they had the resources to make this commitment.

The elders suggested they respond to one request at a time from the school instead of initially adopting the school without a clear understanding of the commitment. The members agreed to this approach.

The initial request was to paint a hallway over a weekend. Church members jumped in with enthusiasm and painted the hallway in a few hours. The church is now effectively on ongoing call to serve the school.

The adoption is complete because of low-hanging fruit.

Making the Change/Keeping the Change

Not only does the change itself have to be implemented, that same change must become a part of the church's culture.

And here is the challenging reality: There will always be change to lead. It is a never-ending cycle of introducing change, implementing change, incorporating change, and introducing the next change.

From Reminder to Reality

While I hope this brief review of the entire process of leading change has been helpful, it is my greater prayer that you will become a God-sent agent of change in your church.

If you want to be comfortable, don't lead change in the church.

If you don't want to be criticized, don't lead change in the church.

If you never want to put your paycheck at risk, don't lead change in the church.

And if you never want to make a difference, to go through this life with the same, tame, and lame approaches most church leaders have, don't lead change in the church.

Who Moved My Pulpit?

Do you remember Derek? He is the pastor of Redeemer Church who moved the pulpit. He is the pastor who endured an unbelievable backlash from the members because of something that seemed rather mundane. And he is the pastor who, by his own account, lost two years of leadership momentum at the church.

"Who moved my pulpit?!" he exclaimed.

But the outcry was more than a simple question. It was a cry to disbelief. It was a scream of emotional agony. It was a question with a greater sense of bewilderment beneath it.

Who moved my pulpit?

That's probably not the question you are asking. But you are asking questions about change, effective change in the church to be specific.

Such is the reason I wrote this book. I wanted to provide you with a roadmap more than a formula. I wanted you to understand how some of the best leaders have led change in their churches.

But there is something more here than roadmaps and stages, more than a lecture on leading change.

There is you.

You are the pastor. You are the church staff person. You are an elder. You are a deacon. You are a key lay leader in the church.

Are you ready to make a difference in this brief life whatever the cost? There are tens of thousands of churches in need of a massive infusion of revitalization.

God has called you to lead change for such a time as this.

Be prepared.

Be courageous.

Be a leader of change for the glory of God.

"Haven't I commanded you: be strong and courageous? Do not be afraid or discouraged, for the LORD your God is with you wherever you go" (Josh. 1:9).

Diagnostic and Study Questions

1. How does the parable of the talents in Matthew 25 and Luke 19 relate to leading change in the church?

2. Why is "hope" a necessary partner with "vision" in leading change?

3. Provide some verses from Proverbs that demonstrate change should include an eager coalition. Explain what each of the verses mean.

4. Why does fear in the heart of a leader hinder change dramatically?

CHANGE READINESS INVENTORY FOR CHURCHES[1]

Answer each of the fifty statements about your church by choosing one number. One person, a group of people, or the entire congregation can do this inventory. When more than one person completes the inventory, get averages for the group. You can compare the readiness to change of one group, such as the elders, to another group, such as the entire congregation.

1 = strongly disagree

2 = disagree

3 = uncertain

4 = agree

5 = strongly agree

1. Our church has a strong desire to reach lost and unchurched people.

1   2   3   4   5

2. Our church is *not* stuck on unnecessary traditions.

1   2   3   4   5

3. Many people in our church share their faith regularly.

1   2   3   4   5

4. Many people in our church develop relationships with those who are not in a church.

1   2   3   4   5

5. Our pastor and our other leadership have a passion to reach people with the gospel of Christ.

1   2   3   4   5

6. The members of our church are friendly to outsiders.

1   2   3   4   5

7. Members in our church are very unified. They do *not* tend to argue over minor issues.

1   2   3   4   5

8. An unchurched person would feel very comfortable in our worship services.

1   2   3   4   5

9. Our church has been through significant change in the past five years and responded well.

    1   2   3   4   5

10. There are not many cliques in our church.

    1   2   3   4   5

11. There is a lot of joy and laughter in our church.

    1   2   3   4   5

12. Very few members, if any, would get upset if the order of worship was changed.

    1   2   3   4   5

13. Members in our church do *not* argue over music and worship styles.

    1   2   3   4   5

14. Our worship services are unified and joyous.

    1   2   3   4   5

15. We have many guests each week in our worship services.

    1   2   3   4   5

16. Many of our members invite people to church every week.

    1   2   3   4   5

17. Sharing the gospel is a priority in our church.

    1   2   3   4   5

18. We have not had a major conflict in our church in the past fifteen years.

1   2   3   4   5

19. New members, including new Christians, can get involved in our church immediately.

1   2   3   4   5

20. We pray for non-Christians regularly in our church.

1   2   3   4   5

21. Our church has a clearly understood and embraced vision statement.

1   2   3   4   5

22. Our church members take good care of our facilities.

1   2   3   4   5

23. There are no power groups in our church.

1   2   3   4   5

24. There are no people in our church who bully others to get their way.

1   2   3   4   5

25. The church staff and the laity work well together.

1   2   3   4   5

26. I would be proud to show an unchurched person our church facilities and grounds.

1   2   3   4   5

27. Our preschool and children's area is neat, clean, modern-looking, with relatively new equipment, toys, and furniture.

1   2   3   4   5

28. Our church is safe and secure, especially the preschool and children's area.

1   2   3   4   5

29. We have a very good small groups or Sunday school organization.

1   2   3   4   5

30. At least one-half of our worship attendance is in a small group or Sunday school class.

1   2   3   4   5

31. Our church creates new small groups and Sunday school classes on a regular basis.

1   2   3   4   5

32. A person without a church background would feel comfortable and welcomed in one of our small groups or Sunday school classes.

1   2   3   4   5

33. Our members are willing to change in order to share the gospel more effectively.

1   2   3   4   5

34. Our church leadership regularly encourages us to be willing to give up our comforts for the sake of the gospel.

1   2   3   4   5

35. We do not have divisive business meetings in our church.

1   2   3   4   5

36. Our church members are very prayerful people.

1   2   3   4   5

37. When we begin change, we have a major focus on praying for that change.

1   2   3   4   5

38. Our pastor and other church leaders are clearly visionaries.

1   2   3   4   5

39. The members in our church accept change readily.

1   2   3   4   5

40. We have an effective new members' or entry-point class in our church.

1   2   3   4   5

41. The leadership expects much of our members, and the members expect much of themselves.

1   2   3   4   5

42. Our church members are willing to get uncomfortable to reach people with the gospel.

1   2   3   4   5

43. Our leadership has great relational skills.

1   2   3   4   5

44. We do not have any significant "sacred cows" in our church.

1   2   3   4   5

45. The members in our church seek to be involved in ministry.

1   2   3   4   5

46. We have a healthy process for conflict resolution in our church.

1   2   3   4   5

47. I have personally made some significant changes in my role in the church in the past five years. (If you have been at the church less than five years, reflect on the time you have been at the church.)

1   2   3   4   5

48. I do not dread business meetings in our church.

1   2   3   4   5

49. I believe the church must continue to change in many areas to be relevant and a gospel force in our community.

1   2   3   4   5

50. Our community leaders and employees have a positive view of our church.

1   2   3   4   5

Add the points from all the statements to determine your church's RFC (Readiness for Change) score.

Point Total	Readiness for Change Rating
225–250	RFC 1
200–224	RFC 2
175–199	RFC 3
150–174	RFC 4
125–149	RFC 5
50–124	RFC 6

RFC 1: Your church can handle change exceptionally well. Your church is probably in the top 2 percent in its readiness for change.

RFC 2: Very good potential to handle change. Improvements could be made, but your church is well above the average in its readiness for change.

RFC 3: Above average potential in the church's readiness for change. The church will need to make several improvements to be ready for significant change.

RFC 4: Average potential for change. "Average" is not good, because the average church in America is losing ground in its community. Many improvements are needed if this church really wishes to be around in twenty years.

RFC 5: In the church's current state, change could cause the church to implode. A church with this RFC score is likely a dying church or will likely become a dying church soon. Radical changes are needed, but the congregation does not appear willing to make the changes.

RFC 6: This church is highly resistant to change. With a score this low, it is one of the most change-resistant churches in America. The death of the church is likely near. It is probably time to consider giving the church facilities to a healthier church before the doors close.

Note
1. This survey is also available for download at thomrainer.com.